AI Governance

Applying AI Policy and Ethics through Principles and Assessments

Dr. Darryl J Carlton

DATA—
DRIVEN
AI

www.technicspub.com/ai

Technics Publications
SEDONA, ARIZONA

115 Linda Vista
Sedona, AZ 86336 USA

https://www.TechnicsPub.com

Edited by Jamie Hoberman

Cover design by Lorena Molinari

First Printing 2024

ISBN, print ed.   9781634624459
ISBN, Kindle ed.   9781634624466
ISBN, PDF ed.   9781634624473

Dedication

With the deepest sincerity and utmost admiration, I dedicate this book to the courageous individuals who wage a daily battle against the relentless challenges of mental health. To the valiant warriors who, despite being engulfed by the suffocating darkness, resolutely push forward. To those who drag themselves out of bed and put one foot in front of the other each and every day.

I have suffered regular visits from the Black Dog for my entire adult life. I am paralyzed in fear at the thought of meeting a new human (dogs are ok). There are many days when I cannot get out of bed. There are other days when my productive output is nothing short of machine-like. I cannot engage in small talk, and I really do not understand signals. When it comes to subtle suggestions, a "wink is as good as a punch in the face" for me, and this has created all sorts of issues in the corporate world. I am incapable of playing corporate politics. This very straightforward and honest perspective, I hope, is reflected in this book. My book aims to strip away the hyperbole and to provide you with a very clear path to success.

To all the mental health warriors out there, know that you are not alone in your battles. Your strength, resilience, and unwavering spirit inspire us all. May this book remind you that your struggles are valid, your experiences are real, and your triumphs, no matter how small, are worthy of celebration. Keep fighting the good fight, for you are the true heroes of our time.

Acknowledgments

There is this notion of the "self-made man" (no sexism intended). Very few people ever achieve anything genuinely on their own, even if they claim to do so. When Edmund Hilary scaled Mount Everest to become the first person to do so, he was not alone. Obviously, his final ascent was with Tenzing Norgay, the sherpa, who was roped just a few feet apart. In Norgay's words, *"We went on slowly, steadily. And then we were there. Hillary stepped on top first. And I stepped up after him."*[1] But even that is an understatement of the support that an individual has to become "self-made". John Hunt led the 1953 Everest Expedition and included over 400 people.

Completing this book is not just a personal achievement but a testament to the collective effort and shared experiences of my support team, which includes colleagues, friends, and family. While the words on the pages are mine, they are a reflection of the insights and wisdom we have all gathered over the years. There is a fabled story about Pablo Picasso whipping up a sketch and the surprised client saying, "But that only took you 10 minutes", to which Picasso responded, "No, it took me 40 years of experience and just a few minutes to get it down on paper." This book is the culmination of decades of our shared work and experience, discussions and debate, a milestone that we can all be proud of.

My thanks and appreciation go to my family; my youngest daughter Alexandra who has always believed in me and encouraged me. She is on her way to stardom. My big girl Sage and her beautiful babies; Anya and Rio who give me strength and purpose. The immensely talented and creative Jessica whose beautiful music is often the background against which I am writing, and her daughter Olivia.

My friends have supported me during times of emotional and professional upheaval and have always been ready with a bottle of wine and a fabulous meal. Sometimes ridicule, but always encouragement; Siobhan, who accuses me of being a nerd (I accept that compliment); Gordon, who has been a constant support for over 35 years, a wine connoisseur who tries in vain to teach me the finer points of appreciation. Rene and Meneja, with Ella and Ares, who have supported me through the most challenging personal and emotional times and whose friendship has never wavered. Adis has provided both friendship and intellectual stimulation. There are a great many people to thank: Ann Clay, Steve Wiley, David Bowen, Remko Jacobs, Rhett Sampson, Adam

---

1 Tenzing Norgay and James Ramsey Ullman Man of Everest (1955).

Todhunter, Pratap Patnaikuni, Paul O'Connor, Eugene Fedorchenko, Ross and Katie Gardiner, Guy Hodgkinson, Tony and Steph Ladias—and these are just a few of the people who have traveled with me on this journey.

A special appreciation goes to the team at Pathfindr.ai—my new professional home. Dawid Naude, Nate Buchanan, Lindsay Page, and Laura Hutton. At Pathfindr.ai I have a vehicle to deliver the results of my research and writing, put my thoughts into action, and effect real change.

I cannot overstate how much I have appreciated the support and contribution of Steve Hoberman and his team at Technics Publishers. He took my ugly typed pages and turned them into a thing of beauty. His contribution to the final product is immeasurable. The book would not be the same without their expert guidance, skill, and experience.

Darryl Carlton

darryl.carlton@me.com
May, 2024

Preface

"Beam me up Scotty - there is no intelligent life down here."

Misquoted from Star Trek (1966-1969)

We have all been influenced by science fiction and the search for artificial intelligence. Characters such as the Robot from 'Lost in Space '(1965), crying out "Danger, danger Will Robinson," or the sensational HAL 9000 from Stanley Kubrick's 1968 film '2001: A Space Odyssey' have captured our imagination. Many of our greatest science fiction writers have themselves been outstanding scientists. The gap between science fiction and science reality has always been relatively small. Today, it appears even closer.

Artificial Intelligence (AI) seemingly burst onto the scene in the closing months of 2023, with breakthroughs in large language models (LLMs) leading to Generative AI products like ChatGPT. In reality, AI has been coming for a long time. Achievements in AI have been inconsistent since the 1940s, progressing in periodic bursts that, in hindsight, are aligned with gains in computing's processing power.

This book is for the non-technical manager, company director, and senior leader in business and government. It aims to provide you, the reader, with an understanding of your obligations for governance and oversight of artificial intelligence—either for the technologies you may use in your enterprise or products and services you might offer your customers that use artificial intelligence.

Depending upon your organization's location and operating markets, legislation that outlines your obligations, rights, and responsibilities may or may still need to be put in place. Two things, however, are clear;

1. every country will eventually put legislation in place to establish guardrails for the use and operation of artificial intelligence, and

2. if you offer your product or service in global markets, then you will be governed by the legislation of those markets, not just your home location.

Joe Longo is the Chair of ASIC (Australian Securities and Exchange Commission). ASIC is the government regulator of Australia's markets, incorporating corporate markets, financial services, and consumer credit regulators. On the 31ˢᵗ of January 2024, Joe Longo had this to say about laws governing the adoption and deployment of AI:

> *"Businesses and individuals who develop and use AI are already subject to various Australian laws. These include laws such as those relating to privacy, online safety, corporations, intellectual property and anti-discrimination, which apply to all sectors of the economy"[2].*

While we are not dealing with a completely barren environment, significant approaches to AI governance and oversight are being discussed worldwide. Chief among those is creating and adopting an ethical framework for AI. The AI Ethical Framework encompasses:

- **Human, Social, and Environmental Well-being**: AI should be a lever for positive change, enhancing individuals' quality of life, enriching society's fabric, and nurturing our planet's ecological balance.

- AI systems must be anchored in **Human-Centered Values**, championing the cause of human rights, the richness of diversity, and the sanctity of individual autonomy. In doing so, they become not just tools of convenience or efficiency but instruments that resonate with the fundamental ethos of our existence.

- **Fairness** must be the cornerstone of AI, embodied in systems that are inclusive and accessible to all and transcend barriers and biases. An AI devoid of fairness is a mirror reflecting our past prejudices into the future. We must ensure that AI is a bridge to equality, not a barrier.

- **Privacy Protection and Security** are paramount in an age where data is as valuable as currency. AI systems should be bastions of trust, protecting the sanctity of personal information while safeguarding against breaches that can undermine the very foundations of our digital society.

- **Reliability and Safety** are the hallmarks of any technology that stands the test of time. AI systems should be unwavering in their performance and steadfast in their functions, operating with the precision and purpose they were designed for. This reliability extends beyond mere functionality, ensuring that safety is

---

[2] Keynote address by ASIC Chair at the University of Technology Sydney, 31 January 2024, "we're not there yet: current regulation around AI may not be sufficient" https://asic.gov.au.

embedded in every line of code and every decision made without human intervention.

- **Transparency and Explainability** must cut through the opacity that often shrouds technological advancements. People have an unequivocal right to understand when and how AI impacts them. The ability to discern AI's involvement in our daily interactions ensures that the human element remains informed and empowered.

- **Contestability** is critical, providing a voice to those impacted by AI. There must be clear, efficient avenues for individuals and communities to question and rectify decisions made by AI systems, ensuring that the technology remains a servant, not a master.

- **Accountability** is the thread that ties all these principles together. There must be a clear line of responsibility from the inception of an AI system through its lifecycle. Those who design, develop, and deploy AI must be identifiable and answerable for their creations, with the provision for human oversight ever-present.

Contents

Introduction

Our insights and knowledge come from a wealth of carefully curated sources. However, we've consciously decided to keep direct referencing to a minimum, ensuring that your reading experience remains engaging and unencumbered by excessive citations. After all, our goal is not to create a dense academic textbook but to provide you with an accessible and easily digestible guide explicitly tailored for non-technical managers and company directors like yourself.

Throughout the book, we'll explore the Eight AI Principles, which form the core of our discussion. We have meticulously distilled these principles from a comprehensive analysis of global approaches to AI governance. By adopting and adhering to these principles, your organization will be well-positioned to navigate the complex landscape of AI regulation and remain compliant across most jurisdictions.

Rest assured, when we include quoted passages, we'll provide the necessary references in footnotes, ensuring you have access to the sources should you wish to delve deeper into a particular topic.

We aim to empower you with the knowledge and tools you need to make informed decisions about AI governance within your organization. By presenting this information clearly, concisely, and easily understandable, we can help bridge the gap between AI's technical complexities and the practical considerations of executive decision-making.

So, please sit back, relax, and allow us to guide you through the fascinating world of AI governance. We're confident that this book's insights will prove invaluable as you navigate the challenges and opportunities ahead.

The material utilized as a source for this book includes the following:

- Isaac Asimov's three laws of robotics as presented in "I, Robot" (1950) Doubleday Press, NYC.

- "If You Think AI Is Hot, Wait Until It Meets Quantum Computing", Susan Galer, Forbes magazine, March 21st 2023.

- "The History of Artificial Intelligence" August 28, 2017, Harvard University special edition on artificial intelligence blog, edited by Rockwell Anyoha.

- "The Bletchley Declaration by Countries Attending the AI Safety Summit, 1-2 November 2023": https://www.industry.gov.au/publications/bletchley-declaration-countries-attending-ai-safety-summit-1-2-november-2023.

- "Recommendation of the Council on Artificial Intelligence" OECD Legal Instruments, OECD/LEGAL/0449, 2023.

- "Government Regulation of an AI in Australia" David Jacobsen, Bright Law, 23rd January 2024, https://www.brightlaw.com.au/government-regulation-of-ai-in-australia/.

- "Safe and responsible AI in Australia consultation paper, interim response", 2024, https://storage.googleapis.com/converlens-au-industry/industry/p/prj2452c8e24d7a400c72429/public_assets/safe-and-responsible-ai-in-australia-governments-interim-response.pdf.

- "Australia's AI Ethics Principles", Department of Industry, Science and Resources, 2023.

- "Executive Order on the Safe, Secure, and Trustworthy Development and Use of Artificial Intelligence", October 2023, Joseph R Biden Jr., The White House, Executive Order.

- "Royal Commission into the Robodebt Scheme", Catherine Holmes AC SC, 7th July 2023.

- European Commission, White Paper on Artificial Intelligence - A European approach to excellence and trust, COM(2020) 65 final, 2020.

- Proposal for a Regulation of the European Parliament and of the Council Laying Down Harmonized Rules on Artificial Intelligence (Artificial Intelligence Act) and Amending Certain Union Legislative Acts, 21/4/2021, Parts 1 & 2.

- "Ethically Aligned Design - a vision for prioritizing human well-being with autonomous and intelligent systems" version 2, IEEE Global Initiative, The Institute for Electrical and Electronics Engineers.

As we enter a new digital era, AI principles must be clearly outlined in policy documents and the algorithms shaping our future. The goal for AI should be to improve our lives, keep us safe, and work in harmony with human values. By doing this, we can ensure that technology and humanity progress together, leading to a future of shared success and well-being for all. This book is structured into four parts:

- **Part One: A Brief History of AI.** AI has developed in "fits and starts" with bursts of output over many decades. The development of large language models (LLM) exemplified by ChatGPT has brought AI to the forefront of public consciousness. But to put the current state of AI into context, and to gain insight into where AI is going, we need to understand, at least briefly, where it has come from, and, more importantly what are the milestones that have propelled AI to the point where we are now all using it.

- **Part Two: The Eight Guiding Principles of AI.** Every country is considering how AI will be deployed and what guardrails are necessary to ensure that AI works for our mutual benefit. We can delve back into the science fiction literature and reflect on Asimov's "Three Laws of Robotics" and consider that powerful technologies need rules to protect our communities. In Part Two, I have distilled the leading AI Ethical Frameworks into a consistent set of guiding principles. Furthermore, I have referenced how each of the global frameworks contributes to the Eight Guiding Principles, and what actions you need to take to be consistent with the various global initiatives. The Eight Guiding Principles discussed in this book, if adopted, should ensure that your AI initiatives are consistent with global standards.

- **Part Three: Ethics and AI.** There is a lot of discussion about ethics and AI. The EU AI Act, for example, has enshrined in legislation ethical standards for the development and deployment of AI. All global frameworks express, in one form or another, ethical considerations for AI's use in business and government. In this section, I discuss AI and propose an ethical framework by looking back at a significant ethical failure, the Cambridge Analytica/ Facebook scandal. The ethical question that is posed is: *just because you can do something, should you?*

- **Part Four: Conformance Assessment Checklist.** The European Union has stipulated a conformance assessment leading to CE Certification for the deployment of AI systems into any member country of the EU. Apart from ensuring that your AI solution can be sold or deployed into EU countries, it is critical that you establish an effective governance and oversight model. Senior executives and Board Members are being held to account by regulators for the effectiveness of their governance. In some circumstances executives have been held legally liable for a failure to ensure governance and oversight practices have been followed. This has led, in some cases, to jail time for executives. In others it has resulted in bans from office. This Conformance Assessment will help your organization construct the necessary governance documents to ensure effective oversight of AI in your organization.

One

A Brief History of AI

In the early 20th century, artificial intelligence (AI) seeds were planted not in the sterile confines of laboratories but in the fertile ground of literature and cinema. The journey began with the "heartless" Tin Man from "The Wizard of Oz" and continued with the eerily humanoid robot impersonating Maria in "Metropolis." These fictional narratives, alongside others, laid the cultural foundation for AI, blurring the line between human imagination and technological possibility.

As science fiction flourished, so did the concept of AI, weaving its way through stories of thought-capable beings that have existed since antiquity. This genre frequently pondered the consequences of human creation turning against its creator, a theme poignantly illustrated in Mary Shelley's "Frankenstein" and echoed in later works such as "2001: A Space Odyssey," "The Terminator," and "The Matrix." Yet, amidst tales of rebellion and conflict, the rare narratives of loyal robots like Gort from "The Day the Earth Stood Still" and Bishop from "Aliens" offered a glimpse into the potential for harmony between humans and their creations.

The term "robot" itself was introduced by Karel Čapek in 1921, marking a significant milestone in our linguistic and conceptual relationship with AI. Meanwhile, Isaac Asimov's Three Laws of Robotics emerged as a crucial ethical framework, albeit more celebrated in fiction than in practical AI development, due to its inherent ambiguities.

Three Laws of Robotics

Asimov, a titan of science fiction, introduced the world to the Three Laws of Robotics through his 1942 short story "Runaround." These laws, later embedded in many of his other works, proposed a moral framework for the behavior of robots. The First Law insists that a robot cannot harm a human or, through inaction, allow a human to come to harm. The Second Law requires a robot to obey human orders unless they conflict with the First Law. The Third Law dictates that a robot must protect its own existence as long as such protection does not conflict with the First or Second Law.

These laws became a central theme across Asimov's stories, creating a narrative sandbox to explore the ethical and practical dilemmas of artificial intelligence. Asimov's robots were designed with these laws so deeply ingrained that violating them was unthinkable, serving as a built-in safeguard against the potential threats AI could pose.

Asimov's exploration of robotics wasn't limited to cautionary tales. He delved into the complexities of robots and humans coexisting, the potential for robots to engage in self-preservation, and the ethical implications of robots making decisions that could impact human well-being. This narrative investigation often highlighted the unintended consequences of the Three Laws, providing fertile ground for Asimov and later authors to ponder the evolving relationship between humans and machines.

Despite their fictional origin, the Three Laws have transcended literature, influencing real-world discussions on the ethics of AI and robotics. They are foundational for debates on safely and ethically integrating advanced AI systems into society. Asimov's visionary work not only entertained but also sparked critical discourse on the future of technology, its potential hazards, and the moral responsibilities of its creators. Through his stories, Asimov posited that knowledge and its applications need not lead to destruction but could lead to beneficial advancements if approached with caution and ethical considerations.

The Turing Test

Against this literary and cinematic exploration backdrop, the mid-20th century witnessed a tangible shift. Figures like Alan Turing began to bridge the gap between fiction and reality, proposing that machines could mimic human reasoning and problem-solving. Turing's seminal work laid the groundwork for AI, posing whether machines could think and, ultimately, what it means to be human. This inquiry was further explored in narratives that presented AI as capable of experiencing emotions, thereby challenging our understanding of consciousness and identity.

Alan Turing, a pioneering figure in computing and artificial intelligence (AI), laid the foundation for a transformative journey into machine intelligence. In his ground-breaking 1950 paper, "Computing Machinery and Intelligence," Turing ventured into uncharted territory by asking a provocative question: "Can machines think?" He shifted the discourse from the abstract notion of thought to the practical assessment of intelligent behavior in machinery. This shift led to the formulation of the Turing Test, a method for evaluating a machine's ability to exhibit human-like conversation. Turing's test sidestepped the philosophical dilemma of whether machines could possess minds or thoughts, focusing instead on observable behavior as the benchmark for intelligence.

Turing's early work sparked widespread interest and optimism within the scientific community. He is credited with conducting the first substantial research in machine intelligence, a term he coined, which laid the groundwork for the modern field of AI research. This burgeoning field officially took shape in the summer of 1956 at a landmark workshop held at Dartmouth College, USA. The workshop attendees, many of whom would become leading figures in AI research, were buoyed by the conviction that machines with human-level intelligence would emerge within a generation. Armed with millions of dollars in funding, they set out to turn this vision into reality.

Despite the enthusiasm Turing's work generated, his approach to defining AI through the lens of behavior rather than thought sparked debate among scholars. Russell and Norvig, notable figures in AI, supported Turing's behavior-centric definition of AI but criticized the Turing Test for its anthropocentric benchmark, arguing that the goal of AI should not be to mimic human behavior so closely that it deceives other humans. Similarly, John McCarthy, another luminary in AI, contended that AI's essence was not in simulating human intelligence but in fostering a distinct form of machine intelligence.

Turing's intellectual legacy in AI is profound. He not only posed the seminal question that would guide the field's development but also proposed a pragmatic framework for understanding and evaluating machine intelligence. His vision and inquiries paved the way for the evolution of AI research, shaping the pursuit of machine intelligence in a manner that transcends the mere replication of human thought and behavior, aiming instead for the creation of autonomous entities capable of intelligent action.

Moving Forward

The evolution of AI from the realm of imagination to a field of scientific inquiry illustrates a profound dialogue between fiction and reality. It highlights how our dreams and fears about artificial beings have shaped, and continue to shape, the development of technologies that could redefine the very essence of human existence.

In the mid-20th century, a revolutionary concept began to take shape, rooted deeply in the aspirations and imaginations of those at the forefront of technology and science. This period was marked by rapid advancements in computing and an era that saw the birth of an idea that would forever alter the course of human history—the concept of artificial intelligence (AI). At the heart of this burgeoning field was a question that challenged the essence of human uniqueness: Could machines think?

The journey into the realm of AI formally began with a groundbreaking initiative by Allen Newell, Cliff Shaw, and Herbert Simon. Their creation, the Logic Theorist, emerged as a beacon of possibility, a program designed to emulate the problem-solving capabilities of the human mind. Funded by the RAND Corporation, the Logic Theorist was not merely a sophisticated piece of software but the first embodiment of artificial intelligence. Its presentation at the Dartmouth Summer Research Project on Artificial Intelligence (DSRPAI) in 1956, a historic conference hosted by John McCarthy and Marvin Minsky, marked a seminal moment in the history of AI.

McCarthy envisioned the Dartmouth conference as a grand collaborative effort that would unify and propel the study of machine intelligence. McCarthy, who coined "artificial intelligence" at this gathering, aimed to bring together leading minds from diverse disciplines to forge a path forward for this developing field. Despite the high hopes, the conference struggled to meet McCarthy's ambitious expectations. The informal structure led to a lack of consensus on methodologies, yet, paradoxically, this environment fostered a unanimous belief in the potential of AI. Though not without its shortcomings, the gathering at Dartmouth ignited a flame that would fuel AI research for decades to come.

Following Dartmouth, the field of AI entered a golden era from 1957 to 1974. The advancements in computing during this period were nothing short of extraordinary. Computers have become faster, more affordable, and more widely accessible. They evolved from mere calculators, executing commands without memory, into sophisticated machines capable of storing vast amounts of information and learning from their interactions. This era also witnessed significant improvements in machine learning algorithms, enhancing the ability of computers to tackle complex problems with unprecedented efficiency.

Pioneering projects such as Newell and Simon's General Problem Solver and Joseph Weizenbaum's ELIZA demonstrated the potential of AI not only to solve intricate problems but also to understand and interpret human language. These early successes garnered the attention and financial support of government agencies, notably the Defense Advanced Research Projects Agency (DARPA), which saw the strategic value in machines capable of transcribing and translating spoken language and processing data at high speeds.

The optimism of the time was encapsulated by Marvin Minsky's bold prediction to Life Magazine in 1970, where he proclaimed that within a mere three to eight years, the world would see a machine with the general intelligence of an average human being. Although this prediction proved overly ambitious, the foundational work laid during these years established the pillars upon which modern AI would be built.

The history of artificial intelligence is a tapestry woven from the dreams and discoveries of visionaries who dared to imagine a world where machines could think and learn. From the ancient myths of crafted beings to the philosophers who envisioned thought as mechanical manipulation of symbols, the quest for artificial intelligence is as much a journey of human aspiration as it is of technological advancement. As we stand on the shoulders of these giants, looking forward to the horizon of AI's possibilities, we are reminded that the essence of this quest is the eternal drive to understand what it means to think, to learn, and to be.

The New New Thing

The history of AI is marked by periods of intense enthusiasm and significant breakthroughs, interspersed with episodes of skepticism and reassessment, often referred to as the "AI winters." These cycles reflect the complex interplay between technological possibilities and the practical limitations of contemporary computing resources. The breakthrough in machine learning and the advent of quantum computing represent pivotal moments in AI's evolution, offering unprecedented computational power and the ability to process vast datasets. These advancements have propelled AI from theoretical models to practical applications that are reshaping industries and society.

The Societal Tapestry of AI

AI's integration into society has been transformative, touching every aspect of human life. From enhancing efficiency in industrial processes to enabling personalized learning experiences in education, AI's applications are vast. However, this transformation is not without its challenges. The displacement of jobs due to automation, privacy concerns arising from surveillance technologies, and the ethical implications of decision-making algorithms in sectors like criminal justice underscores the complex relationship between AI and societal well-being.

Ethical Considerations and Future Horizons

The potential of AI to surpass human cognitive abilities introduces profound ethical questions. Issues such as the autonomy of AI systems, the potential for unintended consequences, and the moral responsibility of creators are at the forefront of discussions on AI ethics. These ethical considerations become even more critical as we stand on the cusp of breakthroughs that could see AI achieve general intelligence. The balance between leveraging AI for its immense potential benefits and safeguarding against its risks requires a nuanced approach that prioritizes ethical guidelines, transparency, and accountability.

Real-World and Hypothetical Scenarios

To explore AI's multifaceted impact further, consider additional real-world and hypothetical scenarios that illustrate both the potential benefits and the ethical challenges associated with its broader adoption:

- **Personalized Medicine Through AI:** Envision AI systems that analyze genetic information, lifestyle data, and medical histories to tailor individual treatment plans, potentially revolutionizing healthcare by improving outcomes and reducing side effects. This precision medicine approach, however, necessitates careful consideration of patient data privacy, consent for data use, and mitigating biases in treatment recommendations to ensure equitable healthcare access for all populations.

- **AI-Driven Job Market Transformation:** Imagine a scenario where AI and automation technologies assume roles in industries ranging from manufacturing to legal analysis, significantly enhancing efficiency and productivity. While this transformation could unlock new economic opportunities and free humans from repetitive tasks, it also poses challenges related to workforce displacement, the need for re-skilling initiatives, and the ethical implications of decision-making in hiring practices by AI systems. The key question revolves around how to ensure a fair transition for workers and the equitable distribution of AI's economic benefits.

- **Smart Urban Ecosystems Powered by AI:** Consider smart cities that leverage AI to optimize traffic flow, energy use, waste management, and emergency services, creating more sustainable and livable urban environments. These AI systems could significantly improve quality of life by reducing pollution, enhancing public safety, and ensuring efficient use of resources. However, implementing such systems raises concerns about surveillance, the privacy of citizens, and the potential for exacerbating socioeconomic divides if benefits are not evenly distributed or if access to the technology is limited to affluent areas.

- **Customized Learning Experiences with AI:** Picture AI-powered educational platforms that adapt to each student's learning style, pace, and interests, potentially transforming education by providing personalized learning experiences that enhance student engagement and achievement. While this use of AI could democratize access to quality education, it also necessitates vigilance regarding data protection for minors, the risk of reinforcing existing educational inequalities, and the importance of ensuring that AI systems do not inadvertently introduce biases into the learning content.

- **AI in Enhancing Disaster Preparedness and Response:** Envision AI tools that accurately predict natural disasters, optimize evacuation routes, and coordinate emergency response efforts, thereby saving lives and minimizing economic losses. The deployment of such AI systems could revolutionize disaster management. However, this application requires careful attention to the reliability of AI predictions, the equitable allocation of resources in response efforts, and the ethical considerations in prioritizing aid distribution.

Each scenario underscores the dual-edged nature of AI's impact on society. While AI offers transformative potential across various domains, realizing this potential responsibly necessitates a concerted effort to address the ethical, privacy, and equity challenges accompanying its adoption.

As we navigate the AI odyssey, fostering a global dialogue encompassing diverse perspectives on AI's role in society is imperative. International standards and ethical frameworks for AI governance can ensure that AI technologies are developed and deployed in ways that benefit all of humanity. The journey ahead requires collaborative efforts across disciplines, industries, and borders to harness AI's potential while addressing its challenges. By doing so, we can ensure that AI remains a force for good, enhancing human capabilities and enriching lives while upholding our ethical and moral values.

Existing Legal Frameworks

In the realm of artificial intelligence (AI), we're navigating a landscape where the speed of technological innovation often outpaces the existing legal guardrails. In Australia, the legal infrastructure is already comprehensive, encompassing a spectrum of regulations that apply to AI just as they do to any other field. These regulations touch on various aspects such as privacy, digital conduct, corporate responsibility, intellectual property, and anti-discrimination.

However, the Australian Government's interim report on AI indicates that our current laws need to be fully equipped to address the unique challenges posed by AI preemptively. This gap is particularly evident in areas like the creation of 'deepfakes[3]', which raises questions under consumer law, the deployment of AI in healthcare, which has implications for clinical safety and privacy, and the use of copyrighted material in training AI, which stirs intellectual property concerns.

Understanding that AI in Australia is not an ungoverned frontier is crucial. AI does not operate in a regulatory vacuum. There are existing laws which can and are being applied to AI. For instance, the Federal Court's decision against RI Advice in 2022 for not sufficiently managing cybersecurity risks demonstrates that current legislation is applicable and can be enforced in AI. This enforceability extends to the governance of AI, with ASIC actively reviewing AI's application in critical sectors such as banking and insurance to ensure that companies manage their AI tools responsibly.

---

[3] Deepfake is where AI is used to pretend to be somebody, often a celebrity, in a place, doing or saying things that they did not actually do. We have seen this with deepfakes of Taylor Swift and Donald Trump as just two examples.

Despite the robustness of the current legal frameworks, the critical question remains: *Are these measures adequate for the pace at which AI is evolving?* AI's potential to drive economic growth is significant, with projections suggesting a substantial increase in Australia's GDP by 2030. Yet, alongside economic benefits, we must consider the societal impact, ensuring that the rapid adoption of AI does not inadvertently marginalize or discriminate against any group.

Data poisoning, input manipulation, and algorithmic biases are just a few of the governance challenges that AI entities must address. More is needed for AI systems to comply with existing regulations; they must also be transparent, understandable, and fair in their operations.

Refining AI governance is a continuous pursuit. We must bolster current regulations while remaining responsive to the dynamic nature of AI advancements. We must strive for a regulatory framework that keeps pace with technological progress and ensures that this progress benefits all members of society. "Is this enough?" should guide our ongoing evaluation of AI regulation, prompting us to seek a balance between innovation and ethical responsibility.

Ethical Frameworks for AI

Establishing ethical frameworks and guidelines is paramount in guiding the development of AI technologies. Initiatives like the European Union's Ethics Guidelines for Trustworthy AI and the IEEE Global Initiative on Ethics of Autonomous and Intelligent Systems exemplify efforts to outline principles that ensure AI's alignment with ethical standards, including transparency, justice, and accountability.

The journey towards ethical AI deployment is complex and multifaceted, requiring a multidisciplinary approach encompassing technical, legal, and ethical expertise. By committing to advancing equity and civil rights, policymakers, developers, and stakeholders can steer AI development in a direction that mitigates risks and maximizes AI's potential benefits for society. Ensuring that AI technologies are developed and deployed in a manner that is inclusive, equitable, and respectful of human rights is not just an ethical imperative but a societal necessity that will determine the trajectory of our collective future in the digital age.

TWO

The Eight Guiding Principles of AI

The emergence of artificial intelligence (AI) as a dominant force heralds a transformative shift in our society. As stewards of this potent technology, we must ensure that the development and deployment of AI systems adhere to a set of core principles that prioritize **Human, Social, and Environmental Well-being.** AI should be a lever for positive change, enhancing individuals' quality of life, enriching society's fabric, and nurturing our planet's ecological balance.

AI systems must be anchored in **Human-Centered Values**, championing the cause of human rights, the richness of diversity, and the sanctity of individual autonomy. In doing so, they become not just tools of convenience or efficiency but instruments that resonate with the fundamental ethos of our existence.

Fairness must be the cornerstone of AI, embodied in systems that are inclusive and accessible to all, transcending barriers and biases. An AI devoid of fairness is a mirror reflecting our past prejudices into the future. We must ensure that AI is a bridge to equality, not a barrier.

Privacy Protection and Security are paramount in an age where data is as valuable as currency. AI systems should be bastions of trust, protecting the sanctity of personal information while safeguarding against breaches that can undermine the very foundations of our digital society.

Reliability and Safety are the hallmarks of any technology that stands the test of time. AI systems should be unwavering in their performance and steadfast in their functions, operating with the precision and purpose they were designed for. This reliability extends beyond mere functionality, ensuring that safety is embedded in every line of code and every decision made without human intervention.

Transparency and Explainability must cut through the opacity that often shrouds technological advancements. People have an unequivocal right to understand when and how AI impacts them. The ability to discern AI's involvement in our daily interactions ensures that the human element remains informed and empowered.

Contestability is critical, providing a voice to those impacted by AI. There must be clear, efficient avenues for individuals and communities to question and rectify decisions made by AI systems, ensuring that the technology remains a servant, not a master.

Finally, **accountability** is the thread that ties all these principles together. There must be a clear line of responsibility from the inception of an AI system through its lifecycle. Those who design, develop, and deploy AI must be identifiable and answerable for their creations, with the provision for human oversight ever-present.

In conclusion, as we stand at the frontier of a new digital dawn, AI principles must be etched in policy documents and the algorithms that will define our future. The vision for AI uplifts, protects, and harmonizes, forging a path where technology and humanity march together to a horizon of shared prosperity and collective well-being.

Principle One: Human, Social, and Environmental Well-Being

What: The human, social, and environmental well-being principle in AI ethics states that AI systems should benefit individuals, society, and the environment. AI should benefit all human beings, including future generations, and help address areas of global concern like the United Nations' Sustainable Development Goals (SDGs).

Why: In the era of rapid technological advancement, it is imperative that the development and deployment of Artificial Intelligence (AI) systems be guided by a clear and unwavering commitment to promoting the well-being and flourishing of humans and the environment. This principle serves as a moral compass, ensuring that the transformative power of AI is harnessed not merely for narrow, short-term gains in productivity or economic growth but for the holistic betterment of society and the planet.

As leaders entrusted with the governance and oversight of AI technologies, it is our solemn responsibility to recognize that the true measure of progress in the algorithmic age lies not in the pursuit of abstract metrics but in the tangible improvement of the human condition. By placing human well-being at the forefront of our decision-making processes, we can ensure that the benefits of AI are distributed equitably, mitigating the risks of exacerbating existing inequalities or creating new forms of harm.

Moreover, prioritizing human well-being and environmental flourishing acknowledges our species' intricate interconnectedness with the natural world. As we harness AI's power to drive innovation and efficiency, we must remain mindful of the potential environmental consequences and actively work to develop sustainable, eco-friendly solutions. By aligning our AI initiatives with environmental stewardship goals, we can contribute to preserving our planet's delicate ecosystems and ensure a thriving future for generations to come.

The responsible and ethical use of AI presents an unprecedented opportunity to address humanity's most pressing challenges, from climate change and resource scarcity to healthcare disparities and educational inequalities. By prioritizing human well-being, we can leverage AI's capabilities to drive meaningful progress on these fronts, fostering a more prosperous, innovative, and secure world.

Furthermore, adopting this principle can catalyze a profound shift in the very structure of our institutions, moving us toward more human-centric models of governance, business, and social organization. By placing individuals' needs and aspirations at the center of our AI-driven initiatives, we can create systems that are more responsive, adaptive, and attuned to the diverse realities of the human experience.

In conclusion, prioritizing human well-being and environmental flourishing represents a vital guidepost for the responsible development and deployment of AI technologies. As leaders, we must ensure that this principle is enshrined at the heart of our AI governance frameworks, informing every decision and action we take. By doing so, we can unlock AI's vast potential to serve as a powerful force for good, driving positive change and creating a future in which all members of society can thrive.

How to Uphold this Principle

1. AI system objectives should be identified and justified regarding their beneficial impact. (Australia's AI Ethics Principles, p.1)

2. AI's broader positive and negative impacts on individual, social, and environmental well-being should be accounted for throughout the AI system's lifecycle. (Australia's AI Ethics Principles, p.1)

3. AI policies must advance equity and civil rights, not disadvantage the already marginalized. (Executive Order on AI, p.1)

4. Governments should work with stakeholders to prepare for AI's transformation of work and society, empowering people with the necessary skills, ensuring a fair transition for workers, promoting responsible use of AI at work, and sharing the benefits of AI broadly and fairly. (OECD AI Principles, p.9)

5. AI systems should be designed and operated to respect and fulfill human rights, freedoms, dignity, and diversity. (IEEE Ethically Aligned Design, p.25)

6. Human rights should be part of the ethical risk assessment of AI systems. (IEEE Ethically Aligned Design, p.25)

7. When designing AI systems, the best available and widely accepted well-being metrics should be used as reference points. (IEEE Ethically Aligned Design, p.28).

The "Human, social, and environmental well-being" principle in AI ethics emphasizes that AI should be developed and deployed to benefit individuals, society, and the environment. It aims to harness AI's potential to address global challenges, contribute to the United Nations' Sustainable Development Goals (SDGs), and prioritize human flourishing and prosperity.

Examples

- **AI for Sustainable Agriculture:** AI technologies can analyze satellite images, weather data, and soil sensors to provide farmers with actionable insights, optimizing crop yields while minimizing environmental impact. AI-powered precision agriculture can reduce water use, fertilizers, and pesticides, contributing to SDGs like Zero Hunger and Life on Land. Projects like Microsoft's FarmBeats and the ICRISAT AI-sowing app exemplify how AI can enhance food security and promote sustainable farming practices.

- **AI for Disaster Response:** AI systems could be deployed to manage disaster response efforts. By analyzing real-time data from satellites, drones, and ground sensors, these systems could predict disaster impacts, optimize evacuation routes, and coordinate emergency services. In the aftermath, AI could facilitate damage assessment and recovery planning, ensuring efficient resource allocation. This scenario highlights AI's potential to save lives, reduce economic losses, and enhance community resilience in natural disasters.

- **AI for Accessible Education:** An AI-powered educational platform designed to adapt learning materials to the needs of all students, but particularly those with disabilities or learning challenges, could provide real-time adjustments to text size, contrast, and auditory descriptions for visual content. While showcasing AI's potential to enhance educational accessibility, this scenario also emphasizes the need to consider privacy concerns and inclusive design practices involving diverse stakeholders in the development process.

These examples demonstrate how AI can promote human well-being, social cohesion, and environmental sustainability. By prioritizing these objectives, AI can be a powerful tool in achieving the SDGs and creating a more equitable and prosperous future for all. However, realizing this potential requires a concerted effort from governments, industries, and the global community to develop AI responsibly, ethically, and inclusively, focusing on equitable benefits for all.

References and Sources

1. AI systems should be used for beneficial outcomes for individuals, society and the environment, addressing areas of global concern like the United Nations' Sustainable Development Goals. AI's positive and negative impacts should be accounted for throughout its lifecycle. (Australia's AI Ethics Principles, p.1)

2. Responsible AI use has the potential to help solve urgent challenges while making the world more prosperous, productive, innovative, and secure. (Executive Order on AI, p.1)

3. AI policies must be consistent with advancing equity and civil rights, and not tolerate the use of AI to disadvantage those already denied equal opportunity and justice. (Executive Order on AI, p.1)

4. The U.S. federal government should lead in developing responsible AI safety and security principles with other nations to ensure AI benefits the whole world rather than exacerbating inequities, threatening human rights, or causing other harms. (Executive Order on AI, p.1)

5. Governments should work with stakeholders to prepare for AI's transformation of work and society, empowering people with the necessary skills. They should ensure a fair transition for displaced workers, promote the responsible use of AI at work to enhance safety and job quality, and ensure AI's benefits are broadly and fairly shared. (OECD AI Principles, p.9)

6. Prioritizing human wellbeing and flourishing (eudaimonia) should be the metric for progress in the algorithmic age, with AI systems explicitly honoring human rights and beneficial values. (IEEE Ethically Aligned Design, p.5)

7. Affordable, universal access to AI systems can benefit humanitarian and development issues, increasing individual and societal wellbeing. (IEEE, p.9)

8. AI systems should be designed to respect and fulfill human rights, freedoms, dignity, and diversity; be verifiably safe and secure; and enable traceability for any harm caused. Human rights should be part of AI ethical risk assessments. (IEEE, p.25)

9. AI system designs should prioritize human wellbeing as an outcome, using widely accepted wellbeing metrics as a reference point. (IEEE, p.28)

Principle Two: Human-Centered Values

What: The principle of human-centered values in AI ethics asserts that artificial intelligence should be developed and deployed in alignment with fundamental human rights, dignity, and the broader aspirations of fostering an equitable and democratic society. AI should serve humanity, guided by a solid moral compass rather than mere algorithmic efficiency.

Why: In an age where Artificial Intelligence (AI) is rapidly transforming the fabric of our society, it is of utmost importance that we, as leaders, are accountable for the governance and oversight of these powerful technologies and ensure that AI systems are firmly grounded in human-centered values. This principle serves as an ethical imperative, recognizing that a deep respect for human rights, individual dignity, and the common good must guide the development and deployment of AI.

Firstly, upholding human-centered values in AI is essential for protecting the fundamental rights of every individual. As AI systems become increasingly interwoven into the decision-making processes that shape our lives, from healthcare and education to employment and criminal justice, we must remain vigilant against the potential for these technologies to perpetuate or amplify existing biases and inequalities. By ensuring that AI is guided by ethical principles such as fairness, non-discrimination, and privacy, we can create a society where everyone is treated with respect and dignity regardless of their background or circumstances.

Moreover, prioritizing human-centered values in our AI initiatives can foster trust and loyalty among our customers, employees, and stakeholders. In an era where consumers are increasingly attuned to the social and ethical implications of the products and services they engage with, demonstrating a genuine commitment to ethical AI practices can set our organizations apart, building relationships that transcend mere transactions. By earning the trust of those we serve, we can create a virtuous cycle of growth and success anchored in a shared vision of technology as a force for good.

Perhaps most importantly, upholding human-centered values in AI has the potential to catalyze a profound and positive transformation of our society as a whole. By harnessing the power of AI to address the most pressing challenges facing humanity, from climate change and public health crises to educational inequalities and social injustice, we can contribute to creating a more equitable, just, and sustainable future. AI systems that are designed and deployed with a deep commitment to human flourishing can unlock new opportunities for innovation, creativity, and collaboration, enriching the lives of individuals and communities across the globe. However, realizing this vision of AI as a catalyst for positive societal transformation requires more than just good intentions. It demands a rigorous and ongoing commitment to ethical reflection, stakeholder engagement, and responsible innovation. As leaders, we must ensure that our organizations have the necessary governance structures, accountability mechanisms, and ethical frameworks to guide the development and deployment of AI in a manner that upholds human-centered values at every step of the process.

In conclusion, upholding human-centered values in AI is not merely a nice-to-have or a box to be checked off, but an ethical and strategic imperative for any organization seeking to thrive in the age of intelligent machines. By placing the well-being and flourishing of humanity at the center of our AI initiatives, we can unlock the vast potential of these technologies to drive positive change while mitigating the risks and challenges that come with any transformative innovation. As leaders, we are responsible for ensuring that this principle guides every aspect of our AI governance and oversight, from the boardroom to the front lines of implementation. Only by doing so can we build a future where AI is a powerful force for good, enhancing rather than diminishing the human experience.

How to Uphold this Principle

1. Embed ethical principles deeply within the AI framework, making them an integral part of the development process rather than a mere addendum.

2. Engage in robust risk management, implementing safeguards that respect human dignity and autonomy. This includes proactively addressing potential biases and ensuring human oversight.

3. Foster a culture of ethical AI within organizations, invest in ethical research and development, and cultivate an environment where ethics are the foundation of all AI initiatives.

4. Collaborate globally to establish and adhere to international guidelines, such as those proposed by the OECD, which advocate for AI systems that respect the rule of law, human rights, and democratic values.

5. Engage continuously with stakeholders, including consumers, employees, and the broader community, to ensure that AI development remains aligned with societal values and expectations.

By embracing human-centered values as a guiding principle, we can harness AI's transformative potential to create a future that empowers humanity while steadfastly defending our fundamental rights and dignity. As leaders, we are responsible for championing this cause and steering AI development towards outcomes that uplift and enrich society.

Examples

- **AI-driven recruitment processes:** AI-driven recruitment processes that are transparent, impartial, and zealously guard privacy. AI solutions must be designed to uphold human-centered values by ensuring fairness, eliminating bias, and protecting the privacy rights of job applicants. By prioritizing ethics in AI-driven hiring, organizations can differentiate themselves in the competitive talent market and build trust with stakeholders.

- **Ethical research and development**: A deep-seated investment in ethical research and the development of AI, pushing the boundaries of what is possible within the ethical and moral framework (Part 3 will have a broader discussion on ethics). Organizations must prioritize ethical considerations throughout the AI development process, from conceptualization to deployment. Organizations can ensure that AI technologies align with human-centered values and contribute to positive societal outcomes by conducting research and development within an ethical framework.

- **Global cooperation and international guidelines:** Global cooperation in pursuing ethical AI, citing international guidelines such as those proposed by the OECD, IEEE, and the multi-country Bletchley Agreement. Collaboration among nations and adherence to shared principles can help embed respect for the rule of law, human rights, and democratic values within AI systems. By working together and following established guidelines, the global community can create AI technologies prioritizing human dignity, autonomy, and well-being.

These examples demonstrate how the principle of human-centered values can be applied in practice, from specific use cases like AI-driven recruitment to broader initiatives like ethical research and development, and global cooperation. By anchoring AI development and deployment in ethical principles and human-centered values, we can harness AI's transformative potential to create a more equitable, just, and sustainable future for all.

References and Sources

1. AI systems should be aligned with human values, serving humans and not vice versa. They should enable an equitable and democratic society by respecting and promoting human rights, diversity, freedom and autonomy, and environmental protection. (Australia's AI Ethics Principles, p.1)

2. Human rights risks need careful consideration, as AI can enable and hamper fundamental rights. Interference with specific human rights is permissible if reasonable, necessary, and proportionate. (Australia's AI Ethics Principles, p.1)

3. People interacting with AI should maintain full, effective control over themselves. AI should not undermine democracy or individual autonomy through deception, unfair manipulation, unjustified surveillance, or misalignment between disclosed purpose and true action. (Australia's AI Ethics Principles, p.1)

4. AI systems should augment, complement, and empower human cognitive, social, and cultural skills. Organizations involved with AI should hire diverse staff to ensure wide-ranging perspectives and minimize the risk of overlooking important considerations. (Australia's AI Ethics Principles, p.1)

5. Irresponsibly deployed AI has deepened discrimination and bias, intensified inequities, caused new harmful discrimination, and exacerbated online and physical harms rather than improving quality of life. (Executive Order on AI, p.1)

6. Throughout their lifecycle, AI systems should respect the rule of law, human rights, and democratic values, including freedom, dignity, autonomy, privacy, data protection, non-discrimination, equality, diversity, fairness, social justice, and internationally recognized labor rights. (OECD AI Principles, p.7)

7. AI actors should implement appropriate mechanisms and safeguards, such as human oversight, that are context-appropriate and consistent with the state of the art. (OECD AI Principles, p.7)

Principle Three: Fairness

What: The principle of fairness in AI aims to ensure that AI systems are inclusive, equitable, and do not perpetuate or exacerbate societal injustices. It requires AI systems to be designed and operated to allow all individuals to access and benefit from the related products or services, regardless of age, disability, race, sex, intersex status, gender identity, or sexual orientation. AI systems must also comply with anti-discrimination laws and enable inclusion throughout their entire lifecycle.

Why: In the grand tapestry of our modern world, where the threads of artificial intelligence (AI) are increasingly interwoven into the fabric of our daily lives, there is a principle that must remain as a guiding light for all those who hold the reins of power and responsibility: the principle of fairness. As leaders entrusted with the governance and oversight of these transformative technologies, our solemn duty is to ensure that the development and deployment of AI systems are rooted in the unwavering commitment to fairness, equity, and justice for all.

Imagine a world where AI systems can operate unchecked without the guiding hand of fairness at the helm. These powerful technologies, which hold the potential to revolutionize every aspect of our lives, from healthcare and education to employment and criminal justice, could quickly become tools of oppression and discrimination. The biases and inequities that have long plagued our society could be amplified and perpetuated, creating a dystopian future where the stain of unfairness tarnishes the promise of AI.

But we can prevent such a bleak outcome. By upholding the principle of fairness in AI, we can ensure that these systems are designed and deployed in a manner that treats every individual with the dignity and respect they deserve, regardless of their race, gender, age, or socioeconomic status. We can create a world where the benefits of AI are accessible to all, where no one is left behind or marginalized by the very technologies that hold the key to unlocking a brighter future.

Moreover, by prioritizing fairness in our AI initiatives, we can ensure that our organizations comply with the myriad anti-discrimination laws and regulations governing our society. Failure to adhere to these legal and ethical standards can result in severe consequences, from costly legal battles to irreparable damage to our reputations. By embedding fairness into the core of our AI systems, we can mitigate these risks and demonstrate to the world that our commitment to equity and justice is more than mere lip service.

However, the importance of fairness in AI extends far beyond legal compliance and risk mitigation. It is a moral imperative, a clarion call to use these powerful technologies as a force for social good. By prioritizing fairness, we can harness the potential of AI to promote social justice, break down the barriers that have long divided us, and create a world where every individual has the opportunity to thrive and reach their full potential.

As leaders, we are responsible for ensuring that the principle of fairness is woven into every aspect of our AI governance and oversight. We must engage in ongoing dialogue with experts in the field, the communities we serve, and the wider public to ensure that our AI initiatives are transparent, accountable, and aligned with the values and aspirations of those we seek to benefit. We must invest in the research and development of fairness metrics and algorithms, and we must be willing to course-correct when necessary to ensure that our AI systems remain true to the principle of equity and justice.

Ultimately, the success of our AI initiatives will not be measured by the speed of our algorithms or the size of our data sets but by the impact we have on the lives of those we serve. By upholding the principle of fairness in AI, we can ensure that this impact is positive and that it uplifts and empowers rather than marginalizes and oppresses. And in doing so, we can help to build a future where the promise of AI is fully realized, where these transformative technologies serve as a beacon of hope and progress for all of humanity.

How to Uphold this Principle

1. Prioritize user-centric design that accounts for the diverse needs and backgrounds of all individuals interacting with the AI system, ensuring equitable access to technologies and services.

2. Engage in appropriate consultation with stakeholders potentially affected by the AI system throughout its lifecycle to identify and mitigate biases early on.

3. Ensure that AI systems provide equitable access and treatment and do not inadvertently disadvantage certain groups due to biased training data or flawed algorithms.

4. Rigorously test and continuously monitor AI systems to identify and address potential biases, especially in high-stakes hiring, housing, and healthcare applications.

5. Adhere to international guidelines and frameworks that promote equitable treatment and access, such as those outlined by the IEEE and OECD.

6. Educate the workforce on ethical AI development and promote public understanding of AI's potential impact on society.

By incorporating fairness into the design, development, and deployment of AI systems, we can work towards technology that empowers all individuals and safeguards against discrimination and bias. This requires ongoing commitment from developers, policymakers, and society at large to identify and address potential biases, engage with diverse stakeholders, and promote equitable access to the benefits of AI.

Examples

- **Voice recognition systems:** A fair AI system, such as a voice recognition system, should be capable of accurately understanding and processing dialects and accents from various ethnic groups and regions. Many of us have seen the humorous video of two Scottish gentlemen trying to use a voice-activated elevator with hilarious results. While funny, as this video was intended, this example highlights the importance of user-centric design in ensuring that AI technologies are inclusive and accessible to all users, regardless of their linguistic or cultural background.

- **AI in urban planning:** Involving community representatives in the design phase of an AI project aimed at urban planning demonstrates the significance of stakeholder consultation in identifying and mitigating potential biases. By engaging with diverse community members, developers can ensure that the AI system addresses the needs of all individuals, not just the majority, promoting fairness and inclusivity.

- **Robodebt scandal:** The Robodebt program in Australia is a cautionary tale of how AI and algorithmic decision-making systems can unfairly treat vulnerable populations. The program's reliance on flawed AI systems without adequate oversight resulted in inaccurate debt claims against welfare recipients. This example underscores the critical importance of fairness, accuracy, and human oversight in AI applications that directly impact people's lives and livelihoods.

These examples illustrate the various aspects of the fairness principle in AI, from designing systems that are accessible and inclusive to engaging with diverse stakeholders and ensuring adequate human oversight to prevent unintended consequences. By learning from these examples, organizations and developers can work towards creating AI systems that prioritize fairness, mitigate biases, and promote equitable outcomes for all individuals in society.

References and Sources

1. AI systems should be fair and enable inclusion throughout their entire lifecycle. They should be user-centric and designed to allow all people interacting with them to access related products or services. This involves appropriate stakeholder consultation and ensuring equitable access and treatment. (Australia's AI Ethics Principles, p.1)

2. There are concerns about AI's potential to perpetuate societal injustices and disparately impact vulnerable and underrepresented groups based on age, disability, race, sex, intersex status, gender identity, and sexual orientation. Measures should be taken to ensure AI-produced decisions comply with anti-discrimination laws. (Australia's AI Ethics Principles, p.1)

3. In the workplace, AI should not be deployed in ways that undermine rights, worsen job quality, encourage undue worker surveillance, lessen market competition, introduce new health and safety risks, or cause harmful labor-force disruptions. (Executive Order on AI, p.1)

4. AI policies must align with advancing equity and civil rights. The U.S. administration will not tolerate AI use that disadvantages those already too often denied equal opportunity and justice. Irresponsibly deployed AI has deepened discrimination and bias, intensified inequities, caused new harmful discrimination, and exacerbated online and physical harms. (Executive Order on AI, p.1)

5. The effectiveness of recommended changes to prevent schemes like Robodebt depends on the will of the government, as culture is set from the top down. (Robodebt Report, p.9)

6. The Robodebt scheme's use of income averaging was essentially unfair, treating many as if they received income when they had not, and creating the fiction

that they owed money back to the government. It subverted the rationale of income support as a safety net. There were also fundamental unfairnesses in placing the onus on recipients to establish earnings from up to five years prior. (Robodebt Report, p.32)

7. Effective AI policies should address safety, privacy, intellectual property rights, human rights, cybersecurity, and public understanding of AI's societal impact. They should support legal norms, develop workforce expertise, attain R&D leadership, regulate for public safety and responsibility, and educate the public. (IEEE Ethically Aligned Design, p.10)

Principle Four: Privacy Protection and Security

What: The principle of Privacy Protection and Security in AI ethics ensures that AI systems respect individuals' privacy, protect data, and maintain robust security measures. This principle encompasses proper data governance and management throughout the AI system's lifecycle, including data anonymization techniques, sound data correlations, and safeguards against unauthorized access and misuse. It also involves identifying potential security vulnerabilities, ensuring resilience to adversarial attacks, and mitigating risks associated with unintended applications and possible abuse.

Why: In the realm of artificial intelligence (AI), where vast troves of data are harnessed to fuel the engines of innovation and progress, there lies a sacred duty that we, as leaders and guardians of this transformative technology, must uphold above all else: the principle of privacy protection and security. Only through an unwavering commitment to safeguarding the intimate details of individuals' lives and ensuring the integrity of the data that flows through our AI systems' veins, can we build a future in which the promise of this technology is fully realized.

Picture, if you will, the consequences of a world in which privacy is treated as an afterthought, where the personal information of countless individuals is left exposed and vulnerable to the whims of those seeking to exploit it for their gain. In such a world, the trust essential to successfully adopting and deploying AI would be eroded and replaced by a pervasive sense of unease and suspicion. The very individuals whose lives we seek to improve through the power of AI would turn away, fearful of the potential for harm that lurks beneath the surface of this technology.

But it is within our power to prevent such a bleak outcome. By placing privacy protection and security at the forefront of our AI initiatives, we can create an environment where individuals feel confident that their personal information is treated with the utmost care and respect. We can foster a culture of trust and transparency in which the benefits of AI are made available to all without fear of compromise or abuse.

We must begin by recognizing the immense responsibility of collecting and processing personal data to achieve this vision. We must implement robust data governance and management practices, ensuring that the information that fuels our AI systems is accurate, representative, and free from the biases and errors that could lead to flawed outcomes. We must be transparent in our data collection and usage practices, providing individuals with clear and concise information about how their personal information is being used and giving them the tools and resources they need to control their data.

However, our privacy protection and security commitment must extend beyond data governance. We must also recognize the inherent vulnerabilities of AI systems and take proactive steps to protect against the ever-present threat of cyber attacks, data breaches, and malicious use. This means investing in developing robust security measures, such as encryption, access controls, and intrusion detection systems, to prevent unauthorized access, manipulation, or exploitation of our AI technologies.

Furthermore, we must be willing to engage in ongoing dialogue and collaboration with experts in privacy and security and the wider public to ensure that our AI initiatives align with the values and expectations of those we serve. We must also be transparent in our efforts to protect privacy and security and willing to course-correct when necessary to maintain our stakeholders' trust and confidence.

Ultimately, the success of our AI initiatives will be measured not only by the benefits they bring to society but also by the degree to which they uphold the fundamental rights and freedoms of the individuals whose lives they touch. By placing privacy protection and security at the heart of our AI governance and oversight, we can ensure that this technology remains a force for good, empowering individuals and communities while safeguarding their intimate details.

In a world where the boundaries between the digital and the physical are increasingly blurred, the principle of privacy protection and security in AI is not merely a nicety but a necessity. It recognizes this technology's immense power and potential and commits to wielding that power responsibly and ethically. Only through such a commitment can we build a future in which AI catalyzes positive change, enhancing the lives of all while respecting the fundamental dignity and autonomy of the individual.

How to Uphold this Principle

1. Implement comprehensive data governance and management practices, including clear data collection, storage, processing, and sharing policies, in compliance with applicable legal frameworks such as GDPR. (Australia's AI Ethics Principles, p.1; EU AI ACT, pp.7-8)

2. Employ data anonymization techniques to protect personal information, such as k-anonymity, l-diversity, and t-closeness, while carefully handling the risk of re-identification. (IEEE Ethically Aligned Design, p.9)

3. Conduct rigorous testing and validation of AI algorithms to ensure sound data correlations and prevent biases or errors that could lead to privacy violations or discriminatory outcomes. (Executive Order on AI in the US, p.1)

4. Implement robust cybersecurity measures, including encryption, access controls, and intrusion detection systems, to protect against unauthorized access and misuse of AI systems and personal data. (Australian Government Response, p.15)

5. Foster a culture of ethical responsibility and transparency, adhering to legal requirements and considering the broader impacts of AI systems on individual privacy rights and societal values. (OECD AI Principles, p.4)

6. Continuously monitor, update, and refine AI systems to adapt to emerging threats and maintain ongoing resilience while collaborating with the cybersecurity community to share best practices and threat intelligence. (EU AI ACT, p.47)

By integrating Privacy Protection and Security principles throughout the AI lifecycle, from design to deployment and ongoing monitoring, we can harness the benefits of AI technologies while mitigating risks and upholding ethical standards. This requires a proactive, multidisciplinary approach that engages all stakeholders, from developers and policymakers to end-users and the wider public, to ensure that AI serves the greater good while respecting individual rights and societal values.

Examples

- **GDPR Compliance:** The General Data Protection Regulation (GDPR) is a global privacy and data protection standards benchmark. Consider a hypothetical example of an AI-driven marketing platform that must effectively anonymize user data and provide transparency about data usage to comply with GDPR. This example demonstrates the importance of adhering to legal frameworks and implementing robust data protection measures to safeguard individual privacy rights when deploying AI systems. In these very early days of AI adoption, we are already witnessing the concerns raised with a need for compliance with the principles of GDPR data protection.

- **Security Vulnerability in AI Healthcare Application:** Imagine a scenario where a healthcare AI application designed to predict patient health outcomes based on personal health data is compromised due to a security vulnerability. This breach could lead to the exposure of sensitive health information or the manipulation of AI predictions, resulting in potentially harmful medical recommendations. This example highlights the critical need for embedding strong security measures and continuous monitoring to detect and mitigate risks associated with AI systems handling sensitive data.

- **Data Anonymization Techniques:** Data anonymization plays a pivotal role in protecting individual privacy. Techniques such as k-anonymity, l-diversity, and t-closeness ensure that individuals cannot be traced or identified from the datasets used in AI systems. However, the text also warns that anonymization must be handled carefully, as poorly anonymized data can sometimes be re-identified through data linkage or de-anonymization attacks (reconstruction of PII). This example underscores the importance of employing effective data anonymization techniques while acknowledging the challenges and risks.

These examples illustrate the multifaceted nature of privacy protection and security in AI systems. They demonstrate the need to comply with legal frameworks, implement robust security measures to prevent breaches and misuse, and safeguard individual privacy by applying data anonymization techniques. By providing these concrete examples, the text contextualizes the principle of "Privacy Protection and Security" and emphasizes its practical implications in developing and deploying AI technologies.

References and Sources

1. AI systems must respect privacy and data protection throughout their lifecycle. This includes proper data governance, management, and anonymization where applicable. The connection between data and AI-drawn inferences should be sound and continually assessed. (Australia's AI Ethics Principles, p.1)

2. Appropriate AI system security measures should include identifying potential vulnerabilities, ensuring attack resilience, accounting for unintended applications and abuse risks, and implementing mitigation measures. (Australia's AI Ethics Principles, p.1)

3. Detailed documentation of AI systems is required, covering the development process, design specifications, system architecture, data requirements, human

oversight measures, validation and testing procedures, risk management, and post-market monitoring. (EU AI ACT, pp.7-8)

4. Americans' privacy and civil liberties must be protected as AI advances. The federal government will ensure lawful, secure data collection, use, and retention that mitigates privacy and confidentiality risks. Privacy-enhancing technologies (PETs) will be used where appropriate. (Executive Order on AI, p.1)

5. The OECD AI Principles complement existing OECD standards on privacy, data protection, digital security risk management, and responsible business conduct. (OECD AI Principles, p.4)

6. Data gathering, cleaning, and processing can lead to harm if datasets use intellectual property without approval, breach laws, undermine commercial interests, or embed biases and errors. (Australian Government Response, p.10)

7. Submissions emphasized embedding national and cyber security measures in AI development and deployment. AI can exacerbate cyber risks but also bolster resilience. Secure-by-design practices should be incorporated from the start. (Australian Government Response, p.15)

8. High-risk AI systems using data-trained models must be developed on training, validation, and testing datasets meeting quality criteria. Appropriate data governance and management practices are required, covering design choices, collection, preparation, assumptions, assessment, bias examination, and gap identification. (EU AI ACT, p.47)

9. Providers of high-risk AI systems may process special categories of personal data to ensure bias monitoring, detection, and correction, subject to appropriate safeguards, technical limitations, and security measures. (EU AI ACT, p.47)

10. High-risk AI systems must comply with established requirements, taking into account their intended purpose and risk management system. (EU AI ACT, p.45)

11. People can define access and provide informed consent regarding their digital data. Mechanisms are needed to help individuals curate their identity and data, with policies informing them of the consequences of information bundling or resale. (IEEE Ethically Aligned Design, p.9)

Principle Five: Reliability and Safety

What: The Reliability and Safety principle in AI ensures that AI systems operate consistently with their intended purpose, accurately reflect their design specifications, and pose no unreasonable safety risks to individuals or society throughout their lifecycle. This principle encompasses the design, development, testing, validation, deployment, and ongoing monitoring of AI systems.

Why: In the brave new world of artificial intelligence (AI), where the boundaries of what is possible are pushed further with each passing day, a principle must serve as the bedrock upon which all our efforts are built: **reliability and safety**. As leaders entrusted with the governance and oversight of these powerful technologies, it is our solemn duty to ensure that the AI systems we develop and deploy are not only innovative and transformative but also dependable and secure, capable of delivering their intended benefits without posing undue risks to individuals, society, or the environment.

Imagine, for a moment, the consequences of an AI system that can operate unchecked without the necessary safeguards and controls in place. In such a scenario, the potential for harm is vast and far-reaching. A self-driving car that fails to recognize a pedestrian, a medical diagnosis system that misinterprets a patient's symptoms, or a financial trading algorithm that makes erroneous decisions—these are just a few examples of the ways in which unreliable or unsafe AI can cause significant damage, not only to the individuals directly affected but also to the fabric of trust that is so essential to the successful integration of AI into our daily lives.

But it is within our power to prevent such outcomes. By upholding the principle of reliability and safety in AI, we can create systems that are robust, resilient, and capable of operating within the parameters for which they were designed. We can instill confidence in the public, demonstrating that the AI technologies we deploy are not only innovative but also trustworthy, capable of delivering their intended benefits without unintended negative consequences.

To achieve this vision, we must begin by recognizing that reliability and safety are not simply boxes to be checked off but fundamental design principles that must be integrated into every stage of the AI development process. From the initial conceptualization and data collection to the testing, deployment, and ongoing monitoring, we must prioritize the creation of AI systems that are transparent, explainable, and accountable, with precise mechanisms in place for identifying and mitigating potential risks.

This requires a multidisciplinary approach that brings together experts from various fields, including computer science, engineering, ethics, and law, to ensure that our AI systems are not only technically sound but also aligned with the values and expectations of the societies they serve. We must engage in ongoing dialogue with stakeholders, including policymakers, regulators, and the wider public, to build trust and foster a shared understanding of the capabilities and limitations of AI technologies.

Moreover, we must recognize that the principle of reliability and safety extends beyond the technical aspects of AI systems. It also encompasses the broader ecosystem in which these technologies operate, including the data that fuels them, the human operators who oversee them, and the societal contexts in which they are deployed. By taking a holistic view of reliability and safety, we can create AI systems that are technically robust and socially responsible, capable of addressing the unique challenges and opportunities presented by the communities they serve.

Ultimately, the success of our AI initiatives will be measured not only by the innovations they bring forth but also by the trust and confidence they inspire in the public. By upholding the principle of reliability and safety, we can ensure that AI remains a force for good, capable of transforming our world in ways that benefit all of humanity while mitigating the risks and challenges that inevitably accompany any new technology.

In a world where the pace of change is accelerating at an unprecedented rate, the principle of reliability and safety in AI is not merely a nicety but a necessity. It recognizes these technologies' immense power and potential and commits to wielding that power responsibly and ethically. Only through such a commitment can we build a future in which AI catalyzes positive change, enhancing the lives of all while safeguarding the well-being of individuals, society, and the planet we share.

How to Uphold this Principle

1. Implement rigorous design and development processes documenting the system's purpose, logic, algorithms, and optimization parameters. This documentation should cover the rationale behind design choices and use pre-trained systems or third-party tools. (EU AI ACT, pp.7-8)

2. Establish a comprehensive risk management system that identifies, analyzes, and evaluates risks associated with the AI system throughout its lifecycle. This should include risks related to everyday use, foreseeable misuse, and other adverse conditions. (EU AI ACT, pp.46-47)

3. Conduct thorough testing and validation of AI systems to ensure they perform consistently and meet the required accuracy, robustness, and cybersecurity levels. Testing should be performed against well-defined metrics and thresholds, considering the system's intended purpose. (Australia's AI Ethics Principles, p.1)

4. Implement continuous monitoring and improvement processes to identify and address issues or deviations in the AI system's performance. This may involve regular updates, adjustments based on new information, and adaptations to changes in the operating environment. (OECD AI Principles, p.8)

5. Develop and adhere to industry standards and best practices for AI reliability and safety, such as the proposed voluntary AI risk-based safety framework in Australia. (Australian Government Response, p.21)

6. Foster a culture of transparency, accountability, and collaboration among all stakeholders involved in developing and deploying AI systems. This includes sharing information on known issues, engaging in public dialogue, and working with policymakers to establish appropriate governance frameworks. (IEEE Ethically Aligned Design, p.34)

By embedding the principle of Reliability and Safety into the entire AI lifecycle, from design to deployment and ongoing monitoring, we can harness the benefits of AI technologies while minimizing their risks and ensuring they remain a force for good in society. This requires a proactive, multi-stakeholder approach that prioritizes public safety, fosters trust, and enables the responsible development and use of AI systems.

Examples

*   **Workplace Automation:** Consider an AI-driven manufacturing robot designed to work alongside humans. The robot's safety mechanisms must be rigorously tested through simulations and real-world trials to ensure reliability and safety. These tests should verify that the robot can detect and respond to human movements, preventing accidents and ensuring a safe working environment. This example highlights the importance of thorough testing and validation in guaranteeing AI systems' reliable and safe operation in practical settings. While the EU AI Act specifically calls out AI embedded in process control machinery

(such as a robot), we should also keep in mind Isaac Asimov's "Three Laws of Robotics" and that robots must do no harm or allow harm to be done.

- **UK Post Office Horizon Scandal:** The UK Post Office Horizon scandal is a poignant case study illustrating the consequences of failing to adequately manage and mitigate risks in complex IT systems. The Horizon system, deployed across the UK Post Office network, was intended to improve efficiency but led to numerous issues, including financial discrepancies and wrongful prosecutions. The scandal revealed several failures in risk management, such as inadequate testing and validation, dismissing user reports of problems, and a lack of transparency and accountability. This example underscores the critical importance of comprehensive risk management throughout an AI system's lifecycle to ensure its reliability and safety.

- **AI Safety Standard Initiative:** Developing a voluntary AI risk-based safety framework in Australia exemplifies industry efforts to translate principles into practical actions. This initiative aims to provide a consolidated, best-practice guide for businesses to navigate the complexities of adopting AI in a manner that prioritizes reliability and safety. By creating a single source of guidance for Australian businesses, this framework helps to operationalize the principle of reliability and safety, promoting the responsible development and deployment of AI systems.

These examples demonstrate the practical implications of upholding the principle of reliability and safety in AI systems across different contexts. They highlight the importance of rigorous testing and validation, comprehensive risk management, and developing industry standards and frameworks to guide the responsible adoption of AI technologies. By learning from these examples, organizations can work towards ensuring that AI systems operate reliably, safely, and in alignment with their intended purposes while minimizing risks to individuals and society.

References and Sources

1. AI systems should reliably operate according to their intended purpose throughout their lifecycle. This includes ensuring they are reliable, accurate, reproducible, monitored, and tested, with ongoing risk management to address identified problems. Responsibility for robustness and safety should be identified. (Australia's AI Ethics Principles, p.1)

2. Detailed documentation of AI systems is required, including development process, design specifications, system architecture, data requirements, human oversight measures, validation and testing procedures, risk management, and post-market monitoring. (EU AI ACT, pp.7-8)

3. Irresponsible AI use could exacerbate societal harms like fraud, discrimination, bias, disinformation, worker displacement, stifled competition, and national security risks. (Executive Order on AI, p.1)

4. AI must be safe, secure, robust, reliable, standardized, and evaluated to mitigate risks. Testing, evaluation, and monitoring ensure intended functioning, resilience against misuse, ethical development, and legal compliance. Effective labeling and provenance mechanisms are needed. (Executive Order on AI, p.1)

5. In the workplace, AI should not undermine rights, worsen job quality, enable undue surveillance, lessen competition, introduce health and safety risks, or cause harmful disruptions. (Executive Order on AI, p.1)

6. AI systems should be robust, secure, and safe throughout their lifecycle, functioning appropriately and not posing unreasonable safety risks even under adverse conditions. Systematic risk management should be applied continuously to address risks. (OECD AI Principles, p.8)

7. The effectiveness of changes to prevent schemes like Robodebt depends on the government's will, as culture is set from the top down. (Robodebt Report, p.9)

8. The National AI Center in Australia will work with the industry to produce a voluntary AI risk-based safety framework for responsible AI adoption in businesses, providing a single source of guidance. (Australian Government Response, p.21)

9. High-risk AI systems must achieve appropriate accuracy, robustness, cybersecurity, and consistency. They should be resilient to errors, faults, inconsistencies, unauthorized alteration attempts, and feedback loops. Relevant accuracy metrics must be declared. (EU AI ACT, p.51)

10. A documented risk management system is required for high-risk AI, continuously identifying, analyzing, evaluating, and adopting measures for known and foreseeable risks throughout the AI lifecycle. (EU AI ACT, p.46)

11. Public awareness of potential AI misuse should be raised in an informed, measured way through education, security awareness, scalability, credibility, and collaboration with government and enforcement to avoid fear. (IEEE Ethically Aligned Design, p.34)

Principle Six: Transparency and Explainability

What: The principle of Transparency and Explainability in AI refer to the ability to understand and elucidate the inner workings of AI systems, including their algorithms, data sources, decision-making processes, and model architectures. Transparency provides clear visibility into these elements, while Explainability focuses on delivering clear and intelligible explanations for AI-driven outcomes and decisions.

Why: In the realm of artificial intelligence (AI), where complex algorithms and vast troves of data intersect to shape the contours of our lives, there is a principle that must serve as a guiding light for all those who hold the reins of power and responsibility: the principle of transparency and explainability. As leaders entrusted with the governance and oversight of these transformative technologies, we must ensure that the AI systems we develop and deploy are not shrouded in secrecy and obscurity but rather open and accessible, capable of being understood and scrutinized by individuals whose lives they touch.

Imagine, if you will, a world where AI operates behind a veil of obscurity, where opaque and inscrutable systems make the decisions that shape the trajectories of our lives, devoid of any semblance of accountability or oversight. In such a world, the trust essential to the successful integration of AI into the fabric of our society would be eroded, replaced by a pervasive sense of unease and suspicion. The very individuals whose lives we seek to improve through the power of AI would be left feeling disempowered and disenfranchised, unable to comprehend or challenge the forces that govern their destinies. But it is within our power to prevent such a bleak outcome. By upholding the principle of transparency and explainability in AI, we can foster a culture of openness and accessibility in which the inner workings of these powerful technologies are laid bare for all to see and understand. We can build bridges of trust between the creators of AI and the individuals whose lives they impact, demonstrating that these systems are innovative, transformative, accountable, and responsive to the needs and concerns of those they serve.

To achieve this vision, we must begin by recognizing that transparency and explainability are not merely abstract ideals but rather concrete and actionable principles that must be woven into the very fabric of our AI systems. From the earliest stages of development to the final moments of deployment, we must prioritize the creation of AI that is open, accessible, and understandable, with clear and concise explanations of how these systems operate and make decisions.

This requires a fundamental shift in how we approach the development and deployment of AI, one that places the needs and concerns of users and affected parties at the center of the process. We must engage in ongoing dialogue with stakeholders, including policymakers, regulators, and the wider public, to ensure that our AI systems are aligned with the values and expectations of the communities they serve. We must be willing to open our processes and methodologies to external scrutiny and validation, demonstrating that our commitment to transparency and explainability is more than mere lip service. Moreover, we must recognize that transparency and explainability are not simply about providing access to information but also about empowering individuals to make informed decisions and take meaningful action based on that information. By providing clear and concise explanations of AI-driven outcomes, we can enable users to challenge results, seek redress when necessary, and hold those responsible for these systems accountable for their actions.

Ultimately, the success of our AI initiatives will be measured not only by the innovations they bring forth but also by the trust and confidence they inspire in the individuals and communities they serve. By upholding the principle of transparency and explainability, we can ensure that AI remains a force suitable and capable of transforming our world in ways that benefit all of humanity while respecting the fundamental rights and freedoms of the individual.

In a world where the boundaries between the digital and the physical are increasingly blurred, the principle of transparency and explainability in AI are not merely niceties but necessities. They are a recognition of these technologies' immense power and potential and a commitment to wielding that power responsibly and ethically. It is only through such a commitment that we can build a future in which AI catalyzes positive change, enhancing the lives of all while safeguarding the dignity and autonomy of the individual.

How to Uphold this Principle

1. Provide clear and comprehensive documentation of AI systems' development processes, including design choices, algorithms, optimization parameters, and pre-trained models or third-party tools. (EU AI ACT, pp.7-8)

2. Ensure that AI systems are accompanied by accessible and understandable instructions, specifying the system's purpose, capabilities, limitations, and potential risks. (EU AI ACT, p.49)

3. Implement mechanisms that allow users to obtain reasonable disclosure regarding AI systems they interact with, including information about key factors and logic used in decision-making. (Australia's AI Ethics Principles, p.1)

4. Commit to responsible disclosure practices, providing timely and meaningful information to foster understanding, enable challenges to outcomes, and promote accountability. (OECD AI Principles, p.8)

5. Develop and adhere to standards that describe measurable and testable levels of transparency, enabling objective assessment and compliance determination. (IEEE Ethically Aligned Design, p.33)

6. Foster a culture of openness and collaboration, engaging in public dialogue, sharing information about AI systems' limitations and appropriate use, and working with stakeholders to establish best practices and governance frameworks. (Australian Government Response, p.20)

7. By embracing Transparency and Explainability, organizations can cultivate trust, mitigate risks, and ensure AI technologies' responsible and ethical deployment. This commitment to openness and clarity serves as a critical differentiator in the age of AI, enhancing brand reputation and contributing to the development of AI that benefits society as a whole.

8. As AI continues to advance and permeate various sectors, Transparency and Explainability will remain essential guideposts. By championing these principles, leaders can navigate the complexities of AI integration and foster an environment where ethical considerations, accountability, and the preservation of human values accompany technological progress.

Examples

Based on the provided text, here are three key examples that describe and elucidate the principle of "Transparency and Explainability" in AI systems:

- **Backward Chaining in Expert Systems:** The concept of "backward chaining" within expert systems is an exemplary illustration of explaining reasoning in AI. In this approach, the system starts with a desired outcome and works backward to determine the steps or rules needed to achieve that goal. For instance, an AI-powered diagnostic system using backward chaining to identify the cause of a medical condition would trace back through a series of rules and logical steps, considering various possible causes and eliminating them until arriving at the most probable diagnosis. By employing backward chaining, the system can provide a transparent and comprehensible explanation of its reasoning, presenting a step-by-step breakdown of the rules, facts, and evidence. This example demonstrates how AI systems can explain the logical steps and regulations to arrive at a particular decision or outcome, fostering transparency, trust, and comprehension between humans and AI. Backward Chaining answers the question, "How did you arrive at that conclusion?"

- **EU AI Act:** The European Union's AI Act is a comprehensive framework emphasizing the importance of transparency and explainability. The legislation mandates that high-risk AI systems be accompanied by detailed documentation (Conformance Assessment) covering various aspects, such as the system's intended purpose, development process, and interactions with other software or hardware. This extensive documentation requirement underscores a commitment to making AI systems understandable and their operations transparent, aiming to foster trust and accountability. By requiring developers to provide clear and accessible information about AI systems, the EU AI Act sets a strong example of how regulatory frameworks can promote transparency and explainability in AI.

- **Robodebt Scheme:** The Robodebt scheme is an example that highlights the importance of transparency and explainability in AI systems deployed in public services. The Robodebt scheme involved automated processes to identify discrepancies in welfare recipient data and raise debts. However, the scheme needed more transparency in its decision-making process, and recipients were given limited information about how their debts were calculated. Several differences exist between the Robodebt scheme and previous manual review processes, such as using averaged income data and placing the onus on recipients to provide contradictory details. This case study illustrates the consequences of a lack of transparency and explainability in AI systems, leading to unfair treatment and an erosion of public trust. It underscores the importance of providing clear explanations, engaging with affected individuals, and ensuring that automated decision-making processes are subject to scrutiny and oversight.

These examples demonstrate the practical implications of upholding the principle of transparency and explainability in AI systems across different domains. They highlight the importance of providing clear explanations of AI reasoning, establishing regulatory frameworks that mandate transparency, and ensuring that AI systems deployed in public services are subject to scrutiny and oversight. By learning from these examples, organizations can work towards developing AI systems that are transparent, understandable, and accountable, fostering trust and promoting responsible deployment of AI technologies.

References and Sources

1. Achieving transparency in AI systems through responsible disclosure is essential for various stakeholders: users, creators, deployers, accident investigators, regulators, legal processes, and the public. Disclosures should be timely, provide reasonable justifications for outcomes, and include key decision-making factors. (Australia's AI Ethics Principles, p.1)

2. People should be able to find out when an AI system engages with them and obtain reasonable disclosure about the system. (Australia's AI Ethics Principles, p.1)

3. General descriptions of AI systems should include purpose, developer, interactions with other systems, software/firmware versions, hardware requirements, user instructions, and installation instructions. (EU AI ACT, p.7)

4. Detailed documentation of AI systems is required, covering the development process, design specifications, system architecture, data requirements, human oversight measures, validation and testing procedures, risk management, and post-market monitoring. (EU AI ACT, pp.7-8)

5. The U.S. federal government will enforce consumer protection laws and enact safeguards against AI-related harms, especially in critical fields. Responsible AI uses that benefit consumers will be promoted. (Executive Order on AI, p.1)

6. AI actors should commit to transparency and responsible disclosure to foster understanding, inform stakeholders of interactions, enable those affected to understand outcomes and allow challenges to outcomes based on plain, easy-to-understand information. (OECD AI Principles, p.8)

7. The effectiveness of changes to prevent schemes like Robodebt depends on the government's will, as culture is set from the top down. (Robodebt Report, p.9)

8. Where automated decision-making is used, there should be a clear review path, plain-language explanations, and available business rules and algorithms for expert scrutiny. A body should be established to monitor and audit automated decision-making processes. (Robodebt Report, p.22)

9. The Robodebt scheme differed from previous data-matching in several ways, including using averaged income data as the primary source, placing the onus on recipients to provide contradictory details, aiming for an automated online process, and extending recovery efforts over several past years. (Robodebt Report, pp.30-31)

10. AI model training can lead to harm if biases and errors are embedded and flow through to outputs. (Australian Government Response, p.10)

11. Transparency measures could include knowing when an AI system is used, public reporting on limitations, capabilities, appropriate use, training data, and data processing. (Australian Government Response, p.20)

12. High-risk AI systems should be designed for sufficient transparency to enable users to interpret outputs. Instructions should include performance characteristics, capabilities, limitations, risks, human oversight measures, and expected lifetime. (EU AI ACT, pp.49-50)

13. Technical documentation for high-risk AI systems should demonstrate compliance and provide necessary information for assessment. (EU AI ACT, p.48)

14. Transparency and accuracy are legally required for governments to use AI. Data, logic, and rules should be accessible to overseers; audit trails and third-party verification are needed, and the public should know who is making ethical decisions. (IEEE Ethically Aligned Design, p.10)

15. New standards should be developed to describe measurable and testable levels of AI transparency for objective assessment and compliance determination. Transparency mechanisms will vary by context. (IEEE Ethically Aligned Design, p.33)

Principle Seven: Contestability

What: The principle of contestability in AI refers to the provision of efficient and accessible mechanisms that allow individuals, communities, and groups to challenge the use or outputs of an AI system, particularly when these outputs significantly impact their lives, rights, or the environment. Contestability ensures that people can question AI-driven decisions and that processes are in place to address their concerns and redress any harm caused.

Why: Where algorithms and data-driven systems hold the power to shape the contours of our lives, there is a principle that must stand as a beacon of responsibility and answerability: the principle of accountability. As leaders entrusted with the governance and oversight of these transformative technologies, we must ensure that the AI systems we deploy are not shrouded in secrecy and impunity but held to the highest standards of transparency, oversight, and liability for their actions and outcomes.

The absence of accountability in AI systems would create a world where the creators and deployers of these technologies could act with impunity, even in the face of clear evidence of bias, discrimination, or harm. In such a scenario, the individuals whose lives are profoundly impacted by these systems would be left without recourse or remedy, their trust and confidence in the promise of AI shattered by the lack of any meaningful mechanism for holding those in power to account. This potential for unchecked power and unintended consequences underscores the critical importance of upholding the principle of accountability in developing and deploying AI technologies.

But it is within our power to prevent such a dystopian future from coming to pass. By upholding the principle of contestability in AI, we can ensure that these systems are innovative and efficient but also fair and accountable, subject to the checks and balances that are the hallmarks of a just and equitable society.

At its core, contestability empowers individuals to challenge decisions that affect their lives, demand transparency and explanations, and seek redress when they believe they have been wronged. It is about ensuring that the rights and freedoms we hold dear—privacy, equality, due process—are not sacrificed on the altar of technological progress but rather safeguarded and strengthened by the systems that promise to transform our world.

To achieve this vision, we must recognize that contestability is not an afterthought or an optional extra, but rather a fundamental design principle that must be woven into the very fabric of our AI systems. From the earliest stages of development to the final moments of deployment, we must prioritize the creation of mechanisms and processes that allow for the contestation and review of AI-driven decisions.

This requires a multifaceted approach, one that encompasses not only technical solutions but also legal and ethical frameworks and robust oversight and governance structures. We must work with policymakers, regulators, and civil society organizations to develop clear and enforceable standards for contestability, ensuring that individuals' rights and interests are protected at every turn.

Moreover, we must recognize that contestability is not a one-size-fits-all proposition but a context-dependent imperative that must be tailored to the specific needs and challenges of each domain in which AI is deployed. In some cases, this may require the establishment of dedicated tribunals or ombudsmen to hear and adjudicate complaints; in others, it may involve the development of user-friendly interfaces and processes that allow individuals to request explanations and lodge appeals quickly.

Ultimately, the success of our AI initiatives will be measured not only by the efficiency and effectiveness of the systems we deploy but also by the trust and confidence they inspire in the individuals and communities they serve. By upholding the principle of contestability, we can demonstrate our commitment to the values of fairness, accountability, and transparency and, in so doing, lay the foundation for a future in which AI is not a source of fear and oppression but rather a tool for empowerment and progress.

In a world where the digital and the physical lines are increasingly blurred, the principle of contestability in AI is not a luxury but a necessity. It is a recognition of the immense power and potential of these technologies and a commitment to wielding that power in a way that respects the fundamental rights and dignities of every individual. It is only through such a commitment that we can hope to build a future in which AI serves not as a master but as a servant of the greater good, working hand in hand with humanity to create a world that is more just, more equitable, and more accessible.

How to Uphold this Principle

1. Provide clear and accessible mechanisms for individuals to challenge AI decisions, such as user-friendly interfaces, dedicated contact points, or independent review bodies. (Australia's AI Ethics Principles, p.1)

2. Ensure sufficient transparency about the information used by algorithms and the inferences drawn, enabling individuals to contest decisions effectively. (Australia's AI Ethics Principles, p.1)

3. Establish oversight mechanisms that incorporate human judgment, particularly for decisions that significantly affect individual rights. This may involve human-in-the-loop approaches or escalation processes for complex cases. (Executive Order on AI, p.1)

4. Develop consistent legal and regulatory frameworks that outline the conditions under which automation in government services can operate, including clear paths for affected individuals to seek review. (Robodebt Report, p.22)

5. Create bodies or expand the powers of existing bodies to monitor and audit automated decision-making processes, assessing their fairness, bias, and usability. (Robodebt Report, p.22)

6. Foster a culture of ethical responsibility within organizations, encouraging the proactive identification and rectification of issues raised through contestability processes. (Principles in Practice section)

7. Continuously monitor and assess the outcomes of AI systems, including any challenges or complaints received, to identify systemic issues and improve the fairness and accountability of these systems over time. (Lessons Learned section)

By embedding contestability into the design, deployment, and governance of AI systems, we can create a future where AI is not only intelligent but also accountable, transparent, and aligned with the values and rights of those it impacts. As AI continues to permeate various aspects of our lives, upholding the principle of contestability will ensure that its benefits are realized ethically and inclusively.

Examples

- **GIGO – Garbage In Garbage Out:** In the early days of data processing, we routinely referred to Garbage In Garbage Out. If the data going in was bad, the reports coming out would also be useless. With the absolute dependence on information technologies, the principle of GIGO has now evolved to **Garbage In Gospel Out** – the computer can never be challenged! The UK Post Office

Horizon scandal serves as a stark illustration of the critical importance of contestability in AI and automated systems. The Horizon system, designed to manage Post Office transactions, inaccurately reported financial shortfalls, leading to the wrongful prosecution and conviction of numerous sub-postmasters. The core issue lies in the incontestability of the system's outputs. Sub-postmasters could not challenge or question the accuracy of the data, as the system was presumed infallible. The Post Office needed to provide effective mechanisms for contesting the system's findings or accessing the information based on these findings. This lack of contestability led to profound injustices and eroded public trust. It highlighted the dangers of blind reliance on automated systems without proper oversight or the ability of affected parties to challenge their outputs.

- **Recommendations for Reform in the Aftermath of the Robodebt Scheme:** The call for contestability is echoed in the recommendations for reform following Australia's Robodebt scheme. These recommendations suggest introducing a consistent legal framework within which automation in government services can operate. The proposed frameworks advocate for transparency about the use of automated decision-making and for making business rules and algorithms available for independent scrutiny. The aim is to ensure that when AI systems significantly impact individuals' lives, there is an effective system of oversight and redress grounded in human judgment and accountability. By embedding contestability into the legal and regulatory frameworks governing AI systems, we can safeguard against the potential harms of automated decision-making and ensure that individuals have avenues to challenge decisions that affect them.

- **Integrating Contestability into AI Development and Deployment:** For senior executives overseeing the integration of AI into their organizations, the principle of contestability offers a roadmap for ethical AI development. It involves designing AI systems with the understanding that their decisions will be subject to scrutiny and challenge. This means creating transparent systems whose decisions can be explained and justified in understandable terms to those affected. It also requires establishing clear procedures for individuals to contest AI decisions and a commitment to address and rectify any issues identified through such challenges. By integrating contestability mechanisms at every stage of AI development and deployment, organizations can foster trust, enhance their reputation, and ensure the responsible use of AI technologies. Contestability becomes not merely a regulatory requirement but a fundamental principle that guides the ethical development, deployment, and governance of AI systems.

- These examples show why it's crucial to have the ability to challenge and question AI systems to ensure they are fair, accountable, and transparent. When people can't contest AI decisions, it can lead to serious problems. But when contestability is built into the design and governance of AI, we can create AI systems that are not only smart but also respect people's values and rights. This helps AI serve the public good in a way that is fair and responsible for everyone involved.

References and Sources

1. Efficient, accessible mechanisms should be provided to allow people to challenge the use or output of an AI system when it significantly impacts a person, community, group, or environment. The 'significant impact' threshold depends on context, impact, and application. (Australia's AI Ethics Principles, p.1)

2. Redress for harm is key to ensuring public trust in AI, with particular attention to vulnerable persons or groups. Sufficient access to algorithm information and inferences is needed for effective contestability. There should be effective oversight with appropriate human judgment for decisions significantly affecting rights. (Australia's AI Ethics Principles, p.1)

3. The U.S. federal government will enforce consumer protection laws and enact safeguards against AI-related harms, especially in critical fields. Responsible AI uses that benefit consumers will be promoted. (Executive Order on AI, p.1)

4. The effectiveness of changes to prevent schemes like Robodebt depends on the government's will, as culture is set from the top down. (Robodebt Report, p.9)

5. Where automated decision-making is used, there should be a clear review path, plain-language explanations, and available business rules and algorithms for expert scrutiny. A body should be established to monitor and audit automated decision-making processes. (Robodebt Report, p.22)

6. The Robodebt scheme extended recovery efforts over several past years based on the flawed notion that discrepancies in previous years indicated recoverable

debts, ignoring that discrepancies didn't necessarily mean overpayments and that reviewed files had likely already yielded the bulk of overpayments. (Robodebt Report, p.31)

7. When AI models are made available to users, potential competition issues become relevant. Dominance of one or few products may create dysfunctional markets with unreasonable pricing, unfair contracts, and unequal access. (Australian Government Response, p.10)

Principle Eight: Accountability

What: Accountability in AI represents a fundamental principle that underpins the ethical deployment and development of AI technologies. It involves fostering a culture of responsibility and ensuring AI systems are developed and used in ways that are just, fair, and beneficial to society. Accountability demands that the relevant organizations and individuals take responsibility for the outcomes of the AI systems they design, develop, deploy, and operate. It encompasses the entire lifecycle of an AI system, from initial conception to eventual decommissioning.

Why: The imperative of accountability in AI stems from the recognition that these technologies are not mere tools but rather powerful agents of change, capable of profoundly impacting every facet of human existence. As AI systems become increasingly interwoven into the fabric of our societies, the potential for these systems to infringe upon the rights and dignity of individuals grows exponentially. In today's world, algorithms make important decisions that affect our lives, such as the news we see, whether we get a loan, what medical treatments we receive, and even the sentences people get in court. If there's no accountability for these algorithms, we'll be powerless against a system that's complex, hard to understand, and impossible to challenge.

But it is within our power to chart a different course, one in which the principle of accountability serves as a bulwark against the potential for harm and injustice. By holding AI actors responsible for the systems they create and deploy, we can foster a culture of ethical and accountable innovation, one in which the development of AI is guided not only by the pursuit of technological progress but also by a deep sense of obligation to the individuals and communities whose lives are touched by these technologies.

Central to this vision of accountability is the notion of answerability – the idea that those who wield the power of AI must be prepared to justify their decisions and actions in the face of public scrutiny and concern. This requires the development of clear and transparent mechanisms for monitoring and auditing AI systems, as well as robust processes for addressing grievances and seeking redress when things go wrong. It means ensuring that there are identifiable entities – be they individuals, organizations, or institutions – who bear the responsibility for the outcomes generated by AI and who can be held to account when those outcomes fail to align with the values and principles we hold dear.

However, accountability in AI is not merely a matter of legal and regulatory compliance but also a profoundly ethical imperative that speaks to our societies' fundamental values. By upholding the principle of accountability, we affirm our commitment to the idea that technology should serve the interests of humanity rather than the other way around. We know that developing and using AI is not the main objective. AI is just a tool that can help us build a society that is better for everyone. The real goal is to create a world where things are more fair and just, where everyone has equal opportunities, and where the needs and dreams of all people are taken into account. AI can be a powerful way to work towards this kind of world, but it's important to remember that AI itself is not the purpose. The purpose is using AI in a way that benefits humanity as a whole and makes life better for all of us. By keeping this perspective in mind, we can ensure that as AI advances, it is guided by our values and used to create a more inclusive, understanding, and caring world for everyone.

Ultimately, the success of our efforts to harness the power of AI for the benefit of humanity will depend not only on the sophistication of our algorithms and the scale of our data but also on the strength of our commitment to the principle of accountability. It is only by ensuring that these technologies are developed and deployed in a manner that is transparent, responsible, and answerable to the people they serve that we can hope to build a future in which AI is not a source of fear and oppression but rather a catalyst for positive change and a testament to the enduring values of our societies.

In this age of unparalleled technological change, the principle of accountability in AI stands as a beacon of hope and a call to action – a reminder that the power to shape our destiny lies not in the hands of machines but in the hearts and minds of those who create and control them. As leaders charged with the weighty responsibility of guiding the development and deployment of AI, we must embrace this principle with unwavering resolve, knowing that the future we build will be the one we deserve – a future in which the promise of AI is fulfilled not through blind faith in technology, but through an abiding commitment to the values that make us human.

How to Uphold this Principle

1. Establish clear organizational roles and responsibilities for overseeing AI safety and ethical compliance, including designated individuals accountable for AI systems' outcomes. (OECD AI Principles, Australia's AI Ethics Framework)

2. Implement appropriate levels of human oversight, particularly for high-risk AI systems, to ensure alignment with ethical standards and the ability to override or intervene in AI decisions as necessary. (EU AI Act)

3. Subject high-risk AI systems to external review by independent oversight bodies equipped to assess compliance with ethical norms and legal standards. (OECD AI Principles)

4. Develop robust legal and regulatory frameworks that clarify liability and accountability issues for AI systems, ensuring avenues for redress when harm occurs. (EU AI Act, IEEE Ethically Aligned Design)

5. Foster multi-stakeholder collaboration, including civil society, law enforcement, insurers, and legal experts, to develop norms and best practices for AI accountability. (IEEE Ethically Aligned Design)

6. Ensure traceability by creating systems for registration and record-keeping that identify the entities legally responsible for an AI system. (IEEE Ethically Aligned Design)

7. Continuously monitor and assess AI systems' outcomes, including any adverse impacts or complaints, to identify and rectify accountability issues. (Australia's AI Ethics Framework)

By embedding accountability into the fabric of AI development and deployment, we can navigate the complexities of this transformative technology while ensuring it serves the greater good. Accountability is not merely a box to be checked but a guiding light that must illuminate every stage of the AI lifecycle, from conception to deployment. As AI continues to shape our world profoundly, upholding the principle of accountability will be essential to realizing its benefits while safeguarding the rights and dignity of all.

Examples

- **The Robodebt scandal in Australia** is a poignant case study illustrating the perils of neglecting accountability in automated decision-making systems. The automated debt recovery system erroneously accused thousands of welfare recipients of owing money, underscoring the dire consequences of inadequate oversight and the absence of precise mechanisms for redress. This scenario vividly demonstrates the need for robust mechanisms to ensure accountability, including legislative reform, transparent decision-making processes, and avenues for those adversely affected to seek review and redress. It highlights the importance of having identifiable parties responsible for AI systems, maintaining human oversight, and enabling external review to prevent and rectify AI-related harms.

- **The OECD Legal Instruments on AI** provides a comprehensive set of guidelines to promote innovative and trustworthy AI while respecting human rights and democratic values. These guidelines emphasize accountability, urging AI actors to be responsible for the proper functioning of AI systems throughout their entire lifecycle. The OECD's approach includes several key components:

  o **Identifiable Responsible Parties:** Advocating for identifying organizations and individuals responsible for AI systems.

  o **Human Oversight:** This section stresses the importance of maintaining appropriate human control over AI systems, particularly when AI decisions directly impact individuals' rights and well-being.

  o **External Review:** Calling for AI systems, especially those with significant potential impact on individual rights, to be subject to external review by independent oversight bodies.

These guidelines offer a valuable framework for ensuring AI development and deployment accountability.

- **The EU AI Act:** The European Union's AI Act represents one of the most ambitious attempts to regulate AI globally. It introduces a risk-based approach to AI governance, outlining specific obligations for high-risk AI systems. Key aspects related to accountability include:

  o **Compliance with Ethical Principles:** Mandating that high-risk AI systems comply with established ethical principles and legal requirements.

  o **Human Oversight:** Requiring high-risk AI systems to incorporate mechanisms for effective human oversight ensures that human operators can override or alter AI decisions.

    o   **Legal Liability:** This section addresses legal implications by clarifying liability and accountability issues and establishing a framework for attributing AI system actions to identifiable legal entities.

The EU AI Act serves as a model for embedding accountability into the legal and regulatory frameworks governing AI. This ensures that the development and use of these technologies align with societal values and protect individual rights.

These examples underscore the critical role of accountability in the ethical development, deployment, and governance of AI systems. They highlight the need for clear lines of responsibility, human oversight, external review, and robust legal frameworks to prevent AI-related harms and ensure that AI serves the greater good. By learning from these examples, organizations and policymakers can work towards building AI systems that are not only innovative but also accountable, trustworthy, and aligned with human values.

References and Sources

1. The principle of accountability aims to acknowledge the responsibility of relevant organizations and individuals for the outcomes of the AI systems they design, develop, deploy, and operate. (Source: Australia's AI Ethics Principles, Australia's Artificial Intelligence Ethics Framework, Department.pdf)

2. Mechanisms should be implemented to ensure responsibility and accountability for AI systems and their outcomes before and after their design, development, deployment, and operation. (Source: Australia's AI Ethics Principles, Australia's Artificial Intelligence Ethics Framework, Department.pdf)

3. Irresponsible use of AI could exacerbate societal harms such as fraud, discrimination, bias, and disinformation, displace and disempower workers, stifle competition, and pose risks to national security. (Source: Executive Order on the Safe, Secure, and Trustworthy Development and Use of Artificial Intelligence.pdf)

4. AI actors should be accountable for the proper functioning of AI systems and respect of ethical principles based on their roles, the context, and the state of the art. (Source: OECD-LEGAL-0449-en.pdf)

5. In the case of the Robodebt scheme, the effectiveness of any recommended change to ensure accountability will depend on the government's will, as culture is set from the top down. (Source: robodebt-full-report.pdf)

6. Recommendations for automated decision-making include legislative reform for a consistent legal framework, clear paths for review, transparency on the use of automation, and establishing a body to monitor and audit automated decision-making processes. (Source: robodebt-full-report.pdf)

7. When AI models deliver outputs, potential harms can be individualized (discrimination, deception, or malice) or manifest at a systemic level (compromising political and social cohesion, stability of labor markets, and human rights). (Source: safe-and-responsible-ai-in-australia-governments-interim-response.pdf)

8. Accountability measures for AI could include designated roles responsible for AI safety, training for developers and deployers, and clear communication when AI is legitimately deployed with high risks. (Source: safe-and-responsible-ai-in-australia-governments-interim-response.pdf)

9. The EU AI Act requires high-risk AI systems to be designed and developed in a way that allows effective human oversight, with measures to enable individuals to understand the system's capabilities and limitations, detect anomalies, interpret outputs, override or intervene in the system's operation, and verify and confirm specific outputs. (Source: EU_AI_ACT_doc1.docx)

10. Legal frameworks should address issues of responsibility, culpability, liability, and accountability for AI systems, considering cultural norms, developing norms and best practices through multi-stakeholder ecosystems, and establishing systems for registration and record-keeping to identify legal responsibility. (Source: IEEE_ethically_aligned_design_v2.pdf)

THREE

Ethics and AI

The Cambridge Analytica scandal, in which the personal data of millions of Facebook users was harvested without their consent and used for political profiling and targeting, represents a complex web of ethical transgressions. At its core, the scandal reveals a profound failure to respect personal privacy and autonomy. However, it also highlights deeper issues around the opacity of AI systems, the potential for data to be misused, and the challenges of holding those who develop and deploy these systems accountable.

Clifford's "Ethics of Belief" (1877) shows how Cambridge Analytica's actions represent a failure to proportion belief to evidence. The company operated on the belief that exploiting user data for political ends was acceptable without any clear ethical justification. It failed to interrogate this belief or consider the potential harm that could result.

Clifford's Ethical Framework

To understand how Clifford's ideas apply to AI ethics, let's revisit the key tenets of his argument. Clifford asserts that we have a moral obligation to ensure our beliefs are based on sufficient evidence. This is not just a matter of intellectual rigor but of ethical duty. He argues that believing something without proper evidence can lead to actions that cause real harm.

In Clifford's view, the shipowner who allows an unfit vessel to sail, believing without firm evidence that it will make the journey safely, is not just making a cognitive error but a moral transgression. The shipowner in Clifford's story must thoroughly investigate the ship's seaworthiness before allowing it to sail. Of course, the moral of this story is that we are all 'the ship owner' in our own endeavors.

Applying this to AI, we can see that developers and deployers of these systems have a moral duty to ensure their 'belief' in the system's safety, fairness, and reliability is grounded in robust evidence. This means rigorous testing, transparent reporting of results, and ongoing monitoring for unintended consequences.

The Importance of Questioning Assumptions

One key lesson of the Cambridge Analytica scandal is the danger of unquestioned assumptions. The company assumed it was acceptable to harvest user data without clear consent, Facebook assumed its data was being used responsibly, and users assumed their personal information was private. All of these assumptions proved to be disastrously wrong.

Clifford's ethics highlight the moral imperative of continually questioning our assumptions, especially when they can impact others. In the context of AI, this means interrogating the values and beliefs embedded in these systems. It means asking tough questions: Is this data representative? Are these algorithms biased? What are the potential misuses of this technology?

Accountability and the Duty of Inquiry

Another critical aspect of Clifford's ethics is the idea that we are morally responsible for the consequences of our beliefs. We are culpable if we believe something without proper inquiry and this leads to harmful actions.

This principle is especially relevant in AI, where the consequences of a flawed or misused system can be far-reaching and profound. For example, the developers of an AI system that wrongly denies people loans or parole cannot escape moral responsibility by claiming they didn't intend these outcomes.

Clifford's ethics suggest that the duty of inquiry is ongoing. It's not enough to test an AI system once and then assume it will always work as intended. Continuous monitoring, refinement, and questioning are required.

Integrating Clifford's Principles into AI Ethics Frameworks

How can Clifford's "Ethics of Belief" be integrated into broader ethical frameworks for AI? I would suggest several key areas:

1. Clifford emphasizes the moral duty of rigorous testing and evidence-based deployment. His ideas underscore that this is not just a matter of good practice but of ethical obligation.

2. Clifford emphasizes the importance of questioning assumptions and interrogating the values and potential biases embedded in AI systems. He reminds us that unquestioned beliefs can lead to harmful outcomes.

3. Clifford's ethics highlight the ongoing nature of the duty of inquiry. They suggest that the moral responsibility to question and verify beliefs is continuous, not a one-time box to be checked.

4. Clifford's framework emphasizes that we are morally responsible for the consequences of our beliefs. In the context of AI, this means that developers and deployers must be held accountable for the impacts of their systems.

5. Clifford's ethics emphasize the human element of AI ethics. They are fundamentally about human responsibility and agency. They remind us that behind every AI system are human choices, beliefs, and moral obligations.

Conclusion

The Cambridge Analytica scandal is a stark reminder of the ethical risks posed by the misuse of AI and big data. But it's also an opportunity to reflect on the deeper philosophical principles that should guide the development and deployment of these powerful technologies.

William Clifford's "Ethics of Belief" offers a compelling moral framework that can inform and enrich our approach to AI ethics. His insistence on the duty of inquiry, the moral imperative of evidence-based belief, and our responsibility for the consequences of our beliefs all have profound relevance in the age of AI.

As we navigate the complex ethical terrain of AI, Clifford's ideas can serve as a lodestar, reminding us of our fundamental moral obligations. They can help us build AI systems that are not just technically impressive but ethically robust - systems that we can believe in, not just because they work, but because they have been rigorously tested, transparently developed, and deployed with a clear-eyed understanding of their potential impacts.

Ultimately, the lesson of Clifford's ethics and the Cambridge Analytica scandal is that the development of AI is not just a technical challenge but a moral one. It requires not just clever algorithms and vast troves of data but a commitment to rigorous inquiry, questioning assumptions, and taking responsibility for the beliefs we embed in our machines. Only by grounding our AI systems in firm ethical principles can we harness their immense potential for good while avoiding the pitfalls of misuse and unintended harm.

Conformance Assessment

Various regulatory frameworks, guidelines, and proposed actions exist to ensure compliance with AI ethics principles and enforce penalties for non-compliance. What has become clear from various court cases in the USA, Canada, and Australia is that organizations' failure to demonstrate adequate plans, governance, and oversight is driving regulators to seek jail terms for executives who have been lax in preparing their organizations for the absolute certainty of cybersecurity breaches and AI challenges.

This section provides you with the tools to complete a self-directed Conformance Assessment.

The EU AI Act emerges as a prominent regulatory framework, laying obligations for high-risk AI systems. These obligations include registration with up-to-date information, conformity assessments involving quality management and technical documentation, and pre-market conformity assessments carried out by providers or notified bodies. The Act also requires high-risk AI systems to have logging capabilities for traceability and monitoring. Non-compliance with these requirements could lead to penalties, though the specific penalties must be detailed in the excerpts.

The OECD's AI Principles and the associated guidance from the Committee on Digital Economy Policy (CDEP) emphasize the importance of regular reporting on the implementation and continued relevance of these principles. While not a direct penalty, this reporting mechanism monitors and encourages compliance among OECD member countries.

Governments, particularly in Australia, increasingly demand proactive steps from companies to ensure AI safety in high-risk contexts. These steps include testing, transparency, and accountability obligations. Some jurisdictions opt for voluntary commitments, while others, like Canada and the EU, are moving towards mandatory requirements for higher-risk AI applications. The Australian Government is considering mandatory safeguards for AI in legitimate, high-risk settings, potentially through amendments to existing laws or new legislation.

Immediate actions proposed in Australia include developing a voluntary AI Safety Standard, exploring options for voluntary labeling and watermarking, and establishing an expert advisory body. Non-regulatory actions are also suggested, such as investing in domestic AI capability, adopting international standards, and leading by example in government use of AI.

New regulatory guardrails are expected to focus on testing, transparency, and accountability. Testing measures could encompass internal and external testing, sharing best practices, ongoing auditing, cybersecurity, and vulnerability reporting. The Australian Government is collaborating with industry to develop an AI Safety Standard, watermarking mechanisms, and an expert advisory group to operationalize safe and responsible AI.

Ongoing efforts across the Australian Government aim to clarify and strengthen laws to safeguard citizens in various domains impacted by AI, such as online safety, automated vehicles, intellectual property, privacy, competition, education, and cybersecurity.

The IEEE's Ethically Aligned Design document suggests that AI system owners register key, high-level parameters, including intended use, training data/environment, sensors, algorithms, interfaces, outputs, and optimization goals. This registration requirement aligns with other frameworks' transparency and accountability principles.

In summary, there is a growing global consensus on the need for robust regulatory frameworks and enforcement mechanisms to ensure compliance with AI ethics principles, particularly for high-risk AI systems. While specific penalties for non-compliance are not detailed in the provided excerpts, the overall trend points towards a mix of mandatory requirements, voluntary commitments, and proactive measures to foster responsible AI development and deployment. Governments, industry, and international organizations collaborate to establish standards, guidelines, and oversight mechanisms to mitigate risks and promote trust in AI technologies.

Section One: AI Systems Overview

Summary of the AI System being Deployed

1. Briefly describe the AI system's objective and functionality.

2. Provide the AI system provider's name, address, contact details, and their authorized representative (if applicable).

3. State the AI system's trade name and any identifying references for traceability.

4. Describe the intended purpose of the AI system.

5. Specify the AI system's current status (on the market, in service, not placed on the market/in service, or recalled).

6. Provide a URL for additional information about the AI system.

7. Provide a general description of the AI system, including:

    a) How the AI system interacts or can be used to interact with external hardware or software (if applicable);

    b) Versions of relevant software or firmware and any requirements related to version updates;

    c) All forms in which the AI system is placed on the market or put into service;

    d) Description of the hardware on which the AI system is intended to run, and whether that is on-premises, cloud, SaaS, or PaaS, naming the providers and locations;

    e) For AI systems that are components of products, provide photographs or illustrations showing external features, marking, and internal layout of those products;

    f) Instructions for use and, where applicable, installation instructions.

Classification of AI System

The EU's Artificial Intelligence Act (AIA) aims to regulate AI systems based on their level of risk to individuals' health, safety, or fundamental rights. High-risk AI systems are permitted on the European market but must adhere to mandatory requirements and undergo an independent Conformity Assessment. The classification of an AI system as high-risk is determined by its intended purpose and the specific modalities of its use rather than solely its function.

High-risk AI systems must comply with legal requirements about data governance, documentation, transparency, human oversight, robustness, accuracy, and security. These requirements align with best practices and international principles to ensure compatibility with AI frameworks adopted by the EU's trade partners.

Low-risk AI systems and those embedded in products or services are not subject to the exact conformity assessment requirements as high-risk systems. However, the harmonization mandate stipulates that embedded AI systems should be held to the same standard as standalone AI systems. As such, low-risk and embedded AI system providers are strongly encouraged to adopt a voluntary code of conduct based on the Conformance Assessment Process as a best practice.

Providers of low-risk AI systems can develop and implement voluntary codes of conduct focusing on their internal procedures and the technical characteristics of the systems they design and deploy. These voluntary codes emphasize process management, allowing organizations to create their guiding principles, adopt guidelines recommended by the European Artificial Intelligence Board, or adhere to industry-specific standards.

By utilizing the Conformance Assessment process, providers of low-risk AI systems can operationalize their commitments to voluntary codes of conduct and enhance their internal quality management systems.

Prohibited Systems

1. **Subliminal Manipulation:** It's prohibited to use AI that manipulates people's behavior through subconscious techniques, especially if it can harm them physically or mentally.

2. **Exploiting Vulnerabilities:** AI cannot be used to exploit vulnerable groups (like those with disabilities or the elderly) in ways that could harm them.

3. **Social Scoring by Authorities:** Public authorities cannot use AI to create 'social scores' based on people's behavior or personality traits, leading to unfair treatment.

4. **Real-Time Biometric Surveillance:** The use of AI for real-time identification of individuals in public spaces by law enforcement is generally banned, except in specific, critical situations (like searching for missing children, preventing imminent threats, or catching serious criminals).

Exceptions for Law Enforcement

1. Be strictly necessary for severe situations like finding missing persons, preventing severe threats, or catching serious criminals

2. Consider the nature and severity of the situation, the potential harm, and the impact on people's rights and freedoms

3. Follow strict conditions and safeguards, including limits on when, where, and on whom it can be used.

High Risk AI Systems

1. **Biometric Identification**: AI is used to identify people through their unique physical features, in real-time or after the fact.

2. **Critical Infrastructure Management**: AI systems that help manage essential services like traffic, water, gas, heating, and electricity to ensure safety.

3. **Education and Training**: AI decides who gets into schools or training programs and assesses student performance.

4. **Employment and Workforce Management:** AI is used to hire, promote, or fire employees, assign tasks, and evaluate their performance.

5. **Public Services Access:** AI that determines eligibility for public assistance, evaluates credit scores, or prioritizes emergency response services like firefighting or medical aid.

6. **Law Enforcement:** AI is used to assess the risk of someone committing a crime, detect emotional states or deepfakes, evaluate evidence reliability, predict crime, and analyze data for crime analytics.

7. **Migration and Border Control:** AI tools for lie detection, assessing risks posed by individuals entering a country, verifying travel documents, and assisting in asylum or visa applications.

8. **Justice and Democracy:** AI systems that support judicial authorities in legal research, interpreting facts and laws, and applying rules to specific cases.

Low-risk AI systems do not process personal data and do not generate predictions or outputs that directly or indirectly impact individuals. These systems typically include industrial applications, such as those used for predictive maintenance, where the AI system analyzes machine data to forecast potential equipment failures or maintenance needs without involving personal information or decisions that could affect people's lives or fundamental rights.

Embedded AI systems are AI components integrated into products or services that are already regulated by other EU legislation, such as toys or medical devices. Although these embedded AI systems are not directly subject to the EU's Artificial Intelligence Act (AIA) requirements, they must still comply with the AIA's provisions due to the harmonization directive. This means that the manufacturers or providers of these products or services must ensure that the embedded AI components meet the same standards and requirements as standalone AI systems covered by the AIA and comply with the specific regulations applicable to their sector.

Section Two: Governance and Oversight

Values and AI Ethical Principles

1. Has the organization defined a set of values to guide the development of AI systems? If yes, please outline these values and norms.

2. Have these values been communicated to external stakeholders and internal AI project team members? Please provide details.

3. Has a governance framework been established for AI projects? If yes, briefly describe how adherence to organizational values will be ensured and demonstrated in practice.

4. Please provide the name and title of the individual responsible for ensuring and demonstrating that AI systems adhere to the defined organizational values.

5. Have the objectives of the AI application been clearly defined and documented? Please summarize these objectives.

6. Has the AI application been assessed against the organization's ethical values? If so, please describe the assessment process and outcomes.

Human Oversight

1. Please describe how the AI system is designed and developed to ensure effective oversight by natural persons during its use, including appropriate human-machine interface tools.

2. Explain how human oversight aims to prevent or minimize risks to health, safety, or fundamental rights that may emerge when the AI system is used as intended or under conditions of reasonably foreseeable misuse.

3. Are the human oversight measures built into the AI system by the provider before it is placed on the market or put into service? If not, are they identified by the provider and appropriate for implementation by the user?

4. Do the human oversight measures enable the assigned individuals to:

   a) Fully understand the capacities and limitations of the AI system, monitor its operation, and detect and address anomalies, dysfunctions, and unexpected performance.

   b) Remain aware of the possible tendency to rely automatically or over-rely on the AI system's output (automation bias).

   c) Can the AI system's output be correctly interpreted, considering its characteristics and the available interpretation tools and methods?

   d) Decide not to use the high-risk AI system or disregard, override, or reverse its output in any situation.

   e) Can humans intervene in the operation of the AI system or interrupt it through a "stop" button or similar procedure?

5. Do the human oversight measures ensure that the user only takes action or decides based on the system's identification if it is verified and confirmed by at least two natural persons?

Considerations for Children

1. Has specific consideration been given to whether children are likely to access the high-risk AI system? If so, please describe the measures taken to address this.

2. Has specific consideration been given to whether the high-risk AI system is likely to impact children? If so, please describe the measures taken to address this.

Section Three: Data and Documentation

Data Usage and Model Development

1. Define the nature of the data used in the AI system (public, proprietary, and private) and state whether it is internal or provided by a third party.

2. Specify how consent has been secured for data use and whether the AI system uses protected attributes.

3. Has the data used to develop the AI application been documented and checked for representativeness, relevance, accuracy, traceability, and completeness? Please provide details.

4. Have the risks identified in the data impact assessment been considered and addressed? Describe the measures taken to handle missing data, imbalanced data, scaling, and normalization.

5. Has the source of the model been documented, and has the selection of the model been assessed for fairness, explainability, and robustness? Please describe the assessment process and outcomes.

6. Have the risks identified in the model been considered and addressed? Please provide a short description of the identified risks and countermeasures.

7. Describe the strategy for validating and testing the model, including performance on extreme values and protected attributes.

8. Have patterns of failure been identified, including backward chaining? Provide a short description of resolving or accounting for key failure modes.

9. Do the training, validation, and testing data sets meet the required quality criteria, including relevance, representativeness, absence of errors, and completeness? Please provide details on the data governance and management practices applied.

10. Describe the measures taken to ensure compliance with data protection principles, such as lawfulness, fairness, transparency, data minimization, accuracy, storage limitation, and security.

11. Outline the processes for handling data subject rights, including providing privacy notices and responding to data subject requests within the required timeframe.

12. Describe the procedures implemented to detect, investigate, report, and communicate data breaches to the supervisory authority and affected data subjects, as applicable regulations require.

Transparency and Provision of Information to Users

1. Please describe how the AI system is designed and developed to ensure its operation is sufficiently transparent, enabling users to interpret and use its output appropriately.

2. Do the AI systems' instructions for use accompany them in an appropriate digital format? Do these instructions include concise, complete, correct, and clear information that is relevant, accessible, and understandable to users?

3. Does the AI system provide key data privacy information to the user on their first interaction, including;

   a) How personal data is collected and how it will be used

   b) How any automated decision making using personal or other data collected will be used

   c) How the data collected by the AI system will be used to monitor employee performance, customer or patient activity

   d) Who will have access to the data which is collected by the AI system, and will this access be provided in the form of 'raw data', extracts or summary and anonymized reporting

   e) For what purpose will persons have access to the data collected

f) Will the data collected by the AI system be anonymized and/or encrypted during its retention

g) Does the AI system provide the opportunity for the user to opt-out without penalty or repercussion

h) How long the data collected by the AI system will be retained, and how it will be destroyed

4. Do the instructions specify the following:

a) What are the identity and contact details of the provider and, where applicable, its authorized representative?

b) What are the characteristics, capabilities, and limitations of the performance of the AI system, including its intended purpose, the level of accuracy, robustness, and cybersecurity against which it has been tested and validated, and any known or foreseeable circumstances that may impact its performance?

c) Are there any known or foreseeable circumstances related to using the AI system that may lead to health, safety, or fundamental rights risks?

d) What is the system's performance regarding the persons or groups of persons on which it is intended to be used?

e) What are the specifications for the input data or any other relevant information regarding the training, validation, and testing data sets used, considering the AI system's intended purpose?

5. Describe the human oversight measures in place, including technical measures to facilitate users' interpretation of AI systems' outputs.

6. What is the expected lifetime of the high-risk AI system, and what maintenance and care measures are necessary to ensure its proper functioning, including software updates?

Section Four: Operations, Risk & Retirement

Model Operations

1. Briefly describe the risks associated with data quality, such as data drift, bias drift, and feature attribution drift.

2. Provide a short description of the risks associated with model decay.

3. Outline the strategy for monitoring and addressing risks related to data quality, drift, and model decay.

4. Explain the organization's strategy for continuously updating the AI application, including the frequency of updates and documentation of model changes.

5. Has a complaints process been established for users of the AI system to raise concerns or suggest improvements? If yes, provide a short description of the process, including the point of contact.

6. Has a problem-to-resolution process been defined for the AI system? If yes, briefly outline the process.

Risk Management Plan

1. Describe the established risk management system for AI systems, including its implementation, documentation, and maintenance, as well as how the risk management system evaluates risks based on the analysis of data gathered from the post-market monitoring system.

2. Explain how the risk management system ensures a continuous iterative process throughout the AI system's lifecycle, including regular and systematic updates.

3. Describe the methods used to estimate and evaluate risks that may emerge when the high-risk AI system is used for its intended purpose and under reasonably foreseeable misuse.

4. Describe how these risks are communicated to the user.

5. Describe the testing process for the AI systems, including how testing identifies the most appropriate risk management measures and ensures consistent performance for the intended purpose. Specify when testing is performed and how preliminary metrics and probabilistic thresholds are defined.

6. Explain how the risk management system specifically considers whether the AI system is likely to be accessed by or impact children.

Retirement and Decommissioning

1. Have the risks of decommissioning the AI system been assessed? Please provide documentation of the identified decommissioning risks and tasks.

2. Outline the strategy to manage the risks associated with decommissioning the AI system, including how data residuals will be handled (e.g., what will happen to data records), model accessibility, and interfaces to other systems.

References and Sources:

1. High-risk AI systems must be registered with specified information that is kept up to date, including provider details, AI system identification, certificate details, declaration of conformity, and electronic instructions for use. (EU AI ACT, p.14)

2. Conformity assessment for high-risk AI systems involves quality management system assessment and technical documentation assessment. The process includes application, documentation, examination, testing, certification decisions, and surveillance. (EU AI ACT, pp.11-13)

3. The OECD's Committee on Digital Economy Policy (CDEP) is instructed to report to the Council on the implementation, dissemination, and continued relevance of the OECD AI Principles five years after adoption and regularly thereafter. (OECD AI Principles, p.4)

4. Governments are increasingly demanding proactive steps from companies to ensure AI safety in high-risk contexts, including testing, transparency, and accountability obligations. (Australian Government Response, pp.4-5)

5. Some jurisdictions have introduced voluntary commitments, while others, like Canada and the EU, are seeking to make commitments mandatory for higher-risk AI through new legal frameworks. (Australian Government Response, p.5)

6. The Australian Government will consider mandatory safeguards for AI in legitimate, high-risk settings where harms are difficult or impossible to reverse through amendments to existing laws or a new legislative framework. (Australian Government Response, p.6)

7. Immediate actions include developing a voluntary AI Safety Standard, options for voluntary labeling and watermarking, and establishing an expert advisory body. (Australian Government Response, p.6)

8. Proposed non-regulatory actions include an AI advisory body, regulatory sandboxes, investing in domestic AI capability, adopting international standards, and government leading by example. (Australian Government Response, p.16)

9. New regulatory guardrails will focus on testing, transparency, and accountability. Testing could include internal and external testing, sharing best

practices, ongoing auditing, cybersecurity, and vulnerability reporting. (Australian Government Response, p.20)

10. The Australian Government is working with industry on an AI Safety Standard, watermarking mechanisms, and an expert advisory group to operationalize safe and responsible AI. (Australian Government Response, p.21)

11. Ongoing work across the Australian Government aims to clarify and strengthen laws safeguarding citizens, including online safety, automated vehicles, IP, privacy, competition, education, and cybersecurity. (Australian Government Response, p.22)

12. The EU AI ACT proposal lays obligations for high-risk AI providers and users, creates legal certainty, promotes trust, strengthens enforcement, and supports innovation through regulatory sandboxes. (EU AI ACT, p.28)

13. Relevant third parties should cooperate with high-risk AI providers and users to enable compliance. Standardization plays a key role in providing technical compliance solutions. (EU AI ACT, p.29)

14. High-risk AI systems are subject to pre-market conformity assessment, generally carried out by the provider, except for remote biometric identification systems requiring a notified body. (EU AI ACT, p.29)

15. Notified bodies for conformity assessment of remote biometric identification AI systems are designated by national authorities based on independence, competence, and absence of conflicts. (EU AI ACT, p.29)

16. High-risk AI systems must have automatic event-logging capabilities to ensure lifecycle traceability, enable monitoring for risks and substantial modifications, and facilitate post-market monitoring. (EU AI ACT, p.48)

17. Owners of AI systems should register key, high-level parameters, including intended use, training data/environment, sensors, algorithms, interfaces, outputs, and optimization goals. (IEEE Ethically Aligned Design, p.31)

AI Readiness Assessment

Most organizations are unsure how to ethically and effectively integrate AI.

This tool will help you to assess your AI readiness.

Based on the research in this book designed to highlight your organization's AI readiness and identify areas for improvement, this self-assessment is your first step towards deploying responsible AI.

With a quick and straightforward process that takes just two minutes, the AI Readiness Assessment is a simple yet effective way to gauge your organization's readiness for AI integration.

- It's completely free.

- Receive customized results instantly.

Scan this QR code or visit the following link for the AI Readiness Assessment.

https://linktr.ee/drdarryl

Index

www.ingramcontent.com/pod-product-compliance
Lightning Source LLC
Chambersburg PA
CBHW080541060326
40690CB00022B/5201